STEAMING INTO TROUBLES

Tales of the Trials and Tribulations of Steam Engine Crews

Michael Clutterbuck

HEDDON PUBLISHING

First edition published in 2022 by Heddon Publishing.

Copyright © Michael Clutterbuck 2022, all rights reserved.
No part of this book may be reproduced, adapted, stored in a retrieval system or transmitted by any means, electronic, photocopying, or otherwise without prior permission of the author.

ISBN 978-1-913166-61-8

Cover design by Heddon Publishing.

Cover image courtesy of the Great Western Trust

This is a work of fiction. Names, characters, businesses, places, events and incidents are either the products of the author's imagination or used in a fictitious manner. Any resemblance to actual persons, living or dead, or actual events is purely coincidental.

www.heddonpublishing.com
www.facebook.com/heddonpublishing
@PublishHeddon

William Harold Clutterbuck
1901 - 1979

Known to his family as Harold and at his work as Bill, our father followed his father, a driver, and his older brother Trevor, into the Great Western Railway. Dad worked in a clerical capacity and passed into British Railways, Western Region, in 1948, retiring, with a gold watch, after forty-five years of railway service in the early 1960s. Being in a 'reserved occupation', he was prevented from joining the army at the beginning of the Second World War, so he joined the Air Raid Precautions service, and we children hardly saw him during the week as he was at work with the GWR during the day and out with the ARP at night. Additionally, he won a medal for his voluntary work in the National Savings Certificate Scheme. Shortly after the end of the War in 1947, our mother left him with three small children, aged ten, eight and four, to bring up on his own, which he managed very well, seeing us all married and off his hands. To our great pleasure, he lived long enough to see all his ten grandchildren, even the two out here Downunder during two visits. He died peacefully in his sleep in his house, looked after by his elder daughter. He was a quiet and patient man who was loved by his children and grandchildren, and also highly respected by his friends and work colleagues.

Introduction

In the 'Steaming Into' series of books, it has been my intention to try and give readers a cursory glimpse into the lives of enginemen in the cabs of steam locomotives over those years in which steam was the mainstay of railway travel. There were many safety devices introduced over the 150 years, yet even at the end of steam in 1968, the working conditions of railway employees in the UK remained poor and, particularly in the cab, could be both demanding and dangerous.

In many ways, the late 1930s were the pinnacle of steam in Britain. The big four major railway companies had been able to iron out their teething troubles after the amalgamations of 1923. Nigel Gresley on the LNER was producing a series of excellent Pacifics, to show that steam trains could match or even surpass the new fast German diesel trains. William Stanier on the LMS was rapidly rejuvenating a whole fleet of locomotives from the parlous state they had been in. Although the Southern Railway was busy electrifying large sections of its network, its later chief engineer Oliver Bulleid was producing remarkable innovations in steam. Even the GWR, often accused of complacency at the time, was producing highly competent new locomotives.

But in spite of these undoubted achievements, the safety and comfort of enginemen was not rated very highly. Coal was commonly broken up and shovelled by human muscles, even in the bigger sheds, until the end of steam; flare lamps with naked flames to peer into the recesses of locomotives were rarely replaced by electric torches; and in mess cabins, weary enginemen put up with wooden benches for a hundred years, so why change this arrangement? Even major safety devices were not always employed. In 1952, a driver passed one signal at caution and two more at danger, resulting in the deaths of over 100 people, with more than 300 injured. In 1906, the GWR had developed a system which prevented this, yet the railways in Britain still have not fully implemented it.

The steam era in the UK ended in Lancashire in July 1968, with the last standard gauge official British Railways steam trains. But the enthusiasm of the general public for steam locomotives can be still seen on any tourist steam railway in Britain today. Steam excursions are even permitted on the regular main lines by special arrangement. Most tourist steam trains are popular, taking their passengers a few miles rumbling along at twenty miles an hour through scenic countryside. I have since travelled in an electric train from Euston to Crewe at well over 100 miles an hour, and this comfortable run was much smoother, yet far less dramatic than racing through Twyford behind a Castle with fourteen on in 1947!

My experience in a steam locomotive cab here in Australia is limited yet very revealing: I was once invited by an ex-colleague to join him in the cab of a tourist locomotive on the narrow gauge 'Puffing Billy', through the Dandenong Ranges near Melbourne. We pulled up at the terminus and I was instructed to climb out and 'put the bag in', to top up the engine's tanks with water. While I was perched on top of the boiler with the flexible hose filling the tanks, I happened to glance down to the platform to see twenty or thirty kids staring up at me, green with envy! Even now, the romance of steam is not dead.

Eagle-eyed readers will observe that, unlike its predecessors, this book contains a couple of stories set in Germany. I make no apologies for this. In the early sixties of the last century, I spent four happy years teaching in Hamburg. I left Germany (accompanied by a very attractive native) with an on-going interest in its railways. There are those who may scoff at the thought of an engine driver escaping from communist East Germany complete with his train, yet it happened, although not quite as I have depicted it. For any reader interested in German railways and who can cope with the German text, the book Geliebte Dampflok by K E Maedel, is well worth perusal.

Finally, I have to express my deep-felt thanks to three people in particular. First to my friend Dr John Ritter who urged me to get my jottings published and who then checked my technical knowledge. To Kath Smith my editor at Heddon, who was brave enough to launch and guide an inexperienced writer, and who has constantly encouraged me with enthusiasm ever since. But above all to my wife Christa, who has put up with my typing, when I ought to have been trimming the hedges or weeding the lawn.

1 - The heavy price of progress (December 1814) 1

2 - The cost of shirked duty (October 1835) 7

3 - It pays to look where you're going! (September 1853) .. 13

4 - First class is not always better (April 1866) 19

5 - A hazardous run to Berlin (January 1872) 25

6 - An old dog knows best (March 1885) 31

7 - A fumble on the Furness (April 1906) 37

8 - A handy tunnel (November 1916) 43

9 - "Pride comes before a fall" (November 1917) 49

10 - "Not my problem now!" (May 1919) 55

11 - A matter of honour (June 1933) 61

12 - Beginning can be difficult (August 1935) 67

13 - A short stint as driver (April 1942) 74

14 - A costly celebration (May 1945) 80

15 - A platform embarrassment (January 1949) 86

16 - Len's luck runs out (February 1951) 92

17 - Ernie Parsons drops a plug (November 1954) 98

18 - Modernisation of the railways (August 1955) 104

19 - A problem with homework (April 1962) 110

20 - A mishap in the cab (October 1993) 117

Glossary of Technical Railway Terms 125

1 - The heavy price of progress (December 1814)

England in 1813 was at war with France, and had been on and off for twenty years, yet while this was of vital importance to workers along the south coast eager to avoid the navy press gangs, it was of little interest to the rest of the population, who did not read newspapers anyway. This was certainly true in the coal mining areas of the north-east of England.

Jem Braithwaite was irritated. "Why can't 'e leave well alone?" he demanded of his mate Harry Thorpe. Both young men were carrying heavy sacks of coal at the railhead at Killingworth colliery. Harry spat a brown stream of tobacco juice onto the gravel.

"Wot's that, Jem?" he asked, "'Oo can't leave wot well alone?"

"'Aven't yer bin lissenin' 'Arry? That new injinwright Stephenson. 'E's bin buggerin' about with 'is fancy machinery instead of getting' on with checkin' the equipment. One o' they pulley ropes snapped yestern and nearly took me leg orf! 'Ow can I do me job with on'y one leg? Me missus and the bairns'd starve if I couldnae work!"

"Well I'm sorry about yer leg, Jem, but I 'eard that Mr Stephenson were tryin' ter mak impruv- impavemin- mak things better fer the company."

"Yer mean improvements?"

"Yeh, that's wot I said."

"Nae yer didn't; yer said - ah well, it don't matter. 'Ow is nearly breakin' me leg an improvement?"

"Yer can be a daft bugger at times, Jem Braithwaite. Mr Stephenson is nae responsible fer ropes; 'is job is lookin' after the pullin' injin. An' I'll tell ye, the pullin' engine's bin workin' much better since 'e came 'ere. 'E knows 'is stuff, does Mr S."

"Yeah, well I'll grant yer that."

"An' I'll tell yer summat else I've 'eard: 'e's workin' on a new type of injin wot don't sit in a shed. It's supposed ter run on the rails and pull the chaldrons along on its own."

"Well there yer go, 'Arry. It's like I said: why can't 'e leave well alone? If 'is injin's so much better, why build a diff'rent one?"

Harry laughed. "Jem, we've bin friends fer a long time an' I'm nae goin' ter fight yer. If yer canna see that, there's nowt I can say ter convince yer! By the way, 'ow did yer 'orse go at Bladon?"

Harry's face lit up. "Yer wouldn't believe it, Jem, I won five shillin'! We et fresh 'addock that day. We even bought shoes fer the bairns who thought it were Christmas! I 'ate ter see chillun runnin' about in bare feet, especially in the snow."

Meanwhile, enginewright George Stephenson was concerned at the increasing cost of horses due to the almost continuous wars with France. He was convinced that a steam-powered engine using cheap coke, instead of expensive corn and hay needed for horses, would lower the costs incurred by the company he worked for. He gazed once more at the drawings on his desk and sighed; there was something at the back of his mind, he knew, but he simply could not put his finger on it. He had prepared the drawing only four weeks ago after studying pictures of the locomotive engines by Trevithick, Blenkinsop and Hedley. He was certain he could improve on them, but the *how* was escaping him. He had already long decided that there was no need for the rack and pinion on the track. Like Richard Blenkinsop, he believed that adhesion alone would suffice to provide enough traction. Indeed, the latter had already produced an engine that could haul ninety tons of coal using adhesion, and another of similar design had been built in Berlin in Prussia, although it had not been successful due to other failings.

One of the problems lay with the iron rails of the plateway: they were not strong enough for the weight they were to carry and tended to break frequently under the loads. He was considering the use of wrought iron instead of cast iron, but worried about the financial loss this might entail, as he had a financial interest in producing of cast iron. Nevertheless, the recently invented wrought iron offered the prospect of more durable rails. It was no stronger than cast iron but was less brittle, especially in very cold weather.

The company produced its own cast iron, so George's

preference for wrought iron meant of course that his company would not benefit from their introduction (history proved him right, and wrought iron became universally accepted).

George's first locomotive was not the first locomotive powered by steam; several other engineers had built successful engines: Hedley, Blenkinsop and Murray. Murray's engine ran on rails with a rack and pinion system to improve adhesion, although in George's opinion this was unnecessary. His first engine was named *Blücher*, after the Prussian general who had arrived at Waterloo in the nick of time to guarantee an allied victory over Napoleon. It proved capable of hauling thirty tons of coal uphill, and even Jem Braithwaite grudgingly admitted that the steam engine had its uses. "Ay, well, I s'pose it c'n beat a 'orse at pullin'."

"Hoi! Jem Braithwaite, coom over 'ere. I wants yer!" Mr Surtees was one of the senior men at Killingworth mine, and an assistant to George Stephenson. Jem stopped what he was doing and walked over. "Yes, Mr Surtees?"

"I wants a smart fellah ter 'elp me with this 'ere engine an' I think you'll do."

"But I know nowt about injins, Mr Surtees."

"Aye, I know that too."

"Well why d'ye want me?"

"'I wants a fellah wot c'n learn. 'An yer c'n read 'an write an' all. Not many others can do that."

The next morning found Jem sitting at a desk, staring at a complex drawing showing a steam locomotive.

"Well, Braithwaite, can yer understand wot yer lookin' at?" Mr Surtees stared at him.

"Er, nae, sir, I cannae understand it."

"Yer've niver seen owt like this before?"

"Nae, sir."

"Coom on, yer've got a brain in yer 'ead, bonny lad. Let me see yer use it. This 'ere's a boiler." A finger outlined the boiler on the drawing. "An' this 'ere's a cylinder fer the steam."

"Aye, I c'n see that."

"An' wot 'appens 'ere?" The finger moved further.

"Er - that's where yer fire 'as ter be, like; where yer shovel the coal in."

"See; I were reet. Y've more'n cabbige between yer ears." Mr Surtees smiled, "I c'n use a man like yerself."

Before he realised exactly what he was doing, Jem found himself employed in the engineering workshop, learning what the various tools were used for, and even (although he would not admit this, even to himself) actually enjoying assembling the parts for a steam locomotive under the direction of an engineer. He learned quickly, and in six months was standing on a wagon, shovelling coal into the firebox of a steam engine, guided by the driver. A year later, he was driving steam engines himself on the colliery line, with another man to shovel the coal into the engine, this time under Jem's, guidance.

By 1818, the colliery had several of George Stephenson's steam engines working hauling the coal tubs, known as chaldrons, down to the loading stages on the river. As a regular driver, Jem was earning much more than he had been as a labourer, and his family had been offered the use of a small house owned by the colliery. His children were better dressed, and even had shoes; in short, the family was comparatively well off compared to their earlier days. Much the same was true of other drivers, who were being seen as something of an elite group in the local community.

Mr Stephenson was kept busy not only maintaining the fleet of engines but also training his young son Robert, to be an engineer too. Instead of sending him to Oxford to become a gentleman, as he could have done, he sent him to Scotland, a world leader in technical training, to undertake basic training as an engineer. The boy had done well, and now assisted his father in developing new designs, when a new challenge emerged.

Over the next few years, Jem Braithwaite learned far more about building steam engines. He became a trusted assistant at the colliery, and even put in an occasional idea about improving or maintaining the rolling stock. His earlier resistance to innovation was gradually disappearing as he saw for himself what the new technology was capable of compared to traditional methods. His respect for his chief grew immensely.

The management of the Liverpool & Manchester Railway had decided that horse haulage would be insufficient for their traffic, and wanted steam locomotives for the purpose; they had opened a competition to see who could offer the most suitable steam engine design and win themselves £500 - a huge reward at the time.

George Stephenson had designed a new type of locomotive engine, which he wanted to enter into the competition; both he and his son Robert had worked on the design and they believed it stood a good chance of winning the £500. The locomotive had been supplied with a blast pipe, which made the fire burn hotter and exhausted the steam more effectively, thus increasing the locomotive's efficiency. They had named their new engine *Rocket*, and the locomotive had even won Jem Braithwaite's approval. Jem had always been conservative (and frequently pessimistic) in his views, and reluctant to see why people should want to improve things that were – in his opinion - working quite satisfactorily. However, even he admitted that the new engine seemed to show its superiority over other locomotives.

The engine was duly entered in the Rainhill trials and, although it was not the fastest engine in the trials, it did fulfil all the conditions set down by the L & M Railway competition, and so won the contract for the Stephensons.

"We'll 'ave these steam injins runnin' all over the country soon," Jem remarked to his old friend Harry when he learned of *Rocket's* success. "There'll be folks knocked over an' killt everywhere!"

His words were prophetic. On the 15th September 1830, the first day of running with the new steam locomotives, crowds filled both sides of the demonstration tracks at Rainhill, to observe the proceedings. There were five locomotives on trial. One of them, *Cycloped*, was powered by a horse on a revolving belt. The other four, including *Rocket*, were steam-powered. The local population was clearly eager to see the free entertainment as the locomotives each performed their duties according to the rules laid down by the company. The winner was to receive the prize, but more importantly, win the contract for providing the locomotives for the company.

Cycloped dropped out of the competition when the horse fell through the drive belt on the floor, to the amusement of the crowd, and then one by one, the other three also failed to complete the tasks required, until only Stephenson's entry *Rocket* fulfilled the requirements. But this engine was shortly to carry out another sad duty.

The spectators saw with horror that the MP for Liverpool, Mr Huskisson, chatting on the parallel track with friends, was knocked down by the approaching Rocket and run over. He was rushed by train towards Manchester, Stephenson himself driving the engine at record speed, but Huskisson's condition worsened and he was taken off near Eccles. Surgeons hurried from Manchester, but were unable to save his life and he breathed his last that evening in a local vicarage surrounded by his wife and friends.

"Wot did I tell yer 'Arry?" Jem asked his friend when he heard the news of the accident.

"Well, I'll 'ave ter admit, you was right this time, Jem," replied Harry, "it's a sad bisnis, but folks'll 'ave ter learn ter tak care on these 'ere railways. They'll 'ave ter put fences along the lines ter keep folk from killin' theirselves."

In the next day's newspapers, the accident was reported as the 'First Death on a Railway'; but what was not reported was that before the Liverpool & Manchester Railway had formally opened, two other people had been killed on the line, and three years earlier on the Stockton & Darlington Railway, a beggar had been killed walking along the track.

But the dangers in this new system of transport were a matter that the public and the authorities were slow to recognise. By the end of 1840, at least a dozen more people had been killed through carelessness as railway lines expanded over the country.

2 - The cost of shirked duty
(October 1835)

Jake Wetherby stared over the wooden laths surrounding the boiler of his 2-2-2 engine as it hauled its train slowly through the saddle in the hills, to begin the long gradient down to the east coast. He was studying the track ahead with unusual care.

"We'll' ave ter keep a sharp eye open 'ere, Arthur," he said to his mate on the footplate, "we're beginning the drop down to t'coast."

"Aye, I'm always a bit worrit comin' down this part of t'line;" replied Arthur Beggs, Jake's 'stoker', as the second man on the footplate was sometimes referred to. Some railways were beginning to use the term 'fireman', while others preferred the idea that the man feeding the fire, like those on the modern small steamships, were normally called stokers. "Whenever we've a heavy train, I'm often afeared o' losin' control downhill." He paused in his shovelling; they had sufficient steam to cope with the next four miles to the next uphill section of the little line, which served several small villages as well as the coal mines in this north-eastern part of the kingdom not far from the big town of Stockton.

Today, they only had a set of three carriages, with few passengers, and one wagon loaded with mixed goods: a box of live rabbits and six boxes of late autumn cabbages, all for the next day's Stockton market, and four loaded coal wagons This was a light train, which would not cause their small engine any serious difficulty on the journey. In fact, the only possible problem they could foresee was that of checking that the track ahead was clear of obstructions, and that any points leading to sidings were set for the main line. Many of the sidings led to local coal mines, and the points were set by employees of the respective mines, who were directed to ensure that they were only set for the sidings when trains were to be sent there for loading. Otherwise, they were to be kept clear for trains using the main line.

Jake and his stoker were always careful to slow down when approaching any of these sidings, so that if the points were not set correctly they could stop in time and reset them. These points were often regarded like country gates, allowing cattle or horses in and out of fields, and of course keeping gates closed had been standard practice among country folk for generations. Even children were well practised in the habit (emphasised if need be by firm physical attention to the back of their heads, or to their behinds).

The day was pleasantly warm; the midday October sun shone on the golden leaves of the horse chestnut trees, under which some children could be seen picking the nuts to throw at each other.

"'Ave yer noticed 'ow the bairns 're playin' with them conkers, these days, Jake?" asked Arthur. "Nae, can't say 'as 'ow I 'ave," responded Jake. "Wot do they do?"

"They drills an 'ole in a nut, 'angs it on a bit o' string, 'an then belts it on another bairn's nut, 'also 'angin' on a bit o' string."

"Wot for?"

"Because they're bairns," laughed Arthur, "that's wot bairns do."

"I've niver seen 'em do anythin' like that."

"It's a new game; I 'adn't seen it afore, neither."

While their train was gently moving along the down grade, the two men were chatting, and keeping an eye open for the coming coal siding. The movable sign showed that it was clear for them to steam through on the main line, and so Arthur bent to check the firebox to see whether he needed to put more coke in for the coming slight uphill gradient. The fire seemed satisfactory, and he stood up again, holding onto the railing which surrounded the two men on the engine's footplate. A quick glance back along the train assured him that the carriages were still rolling along behind the wagonload of mixed goods, which was directly behind the engine. All was still in order, but Jake was careful to lower the regulator, to keep the train's speed to a safe level, bearing in mind that they were on a downhill grade and the engine had no brake. If the train had to stop quickly, he would signal to the brakemen on the rooftops of the carriages, and they would apply brakes on their vehicles to slow and then stop the train.

The two men on the footplate were experienced in their duties and were also well paid for men at their social level. Had it not been for the coming of the new railways, they would have been labourers either on farms or possibly in the coalmines, neither job offering much more than subsistence wages for a man with a family to support. Railwaymen, on the other hand, were relatively well paid if they knew their work, especially if they were footplatemen; such men were valuable, and rewarded accordingly. Jake Wetherby, at thirty-five, was a single man with no dependants, and consequently particularly well-off. Arthur had a wife and two children, but also enjoyed a standard of living higher than he would have expected as a farm labourer or coal miner.

Jake glanced along the coal siding as they passed it, seeing a man loading the three coal wagons from the piles of coal on the staithes, ready for the next coal train to collect them and take them down to the coast for shipping to London, for household fires. The man paused in his shovelling to wave at them as they passed; they returned his greeting. As they passed the siding, the track began its slight upward gradient and Arthur bent once more to check the trim of the fire and put a shovelful of coke into the firebox where he could see a hole in the fire. Jake waited until the cold, wet coke had been burned sufficiently to increase the heat of the fire, then he eased the regulator up to increase its speed in order to tackle the slope with relative ease. Twenty minutes later, they had reached the coast and uncoupled their carriages, before taking the coal wagons further to the jetty, where they could be left for unloading.

Their run back to the railhead in the hills took two-and-a-half hours, and they picked up five more loaded coal wagons from a local coal mine, before moving to the little station where six carriages were waiting. This took longer because there seemed to be an altercation between the station official and an irate passenger.

"I'll go an' see wot the 'ell's that all about," said Arthur stepping off the footplate.

"Nae Arthur," Jake stopped him; "Let 'em sort it out while we 'ave a smoke."

"Ye've got some reet good notions sometimes, Jake, I'll give yer that!"

Both men took out their pipes; it was obvious that the vigorous discussion still had some way to go. Mr Withenshawe, the station official, objected strongly to Fred Haslop demanding to keep his pig with him in the passenger carriage on the grounds that it was a chattel, whereas Geoff Withenshawe claimed that animals were freight, and had to be handled accordingly. Fred pointed out that, apart from the coal trucks, there were no freight facilities on the train, and he wasn't going to let his prize pig sit on coal for the journey to market.

"E'll come out black as pitch and 'e'll be worth nowt!" he said indignantly.

Mr Withenshawe countered that the pig could travel in the carriage with his owner if the said owner were prepared to pay for a seat, and if no other passenger objected to the animal's presence. Most of the passengers saw no problem with this: pigs, goats and ducks commonly travelled with people in their horse-drawn road carriages. However, Mrs Ackroyd, the wife of a wealthy and important landowner refused to travel with 'such a filthy animal' next to her. This caused a further fracas as Fred took issue with her on the hygiene of his pig.

"They should be chargin' us extra fer the intertainment!" muttered one grinning local to his neighbour, "this c'd go on fer ivver!" But it didn't, and finally the matter was settled and Mr Withenshawe signalled to the two footplatemen to start the train.

Arthur tapped out his pipe, checked the pressure gauge and state of the fire, and nodded to Jake, who then opened the regulator lever to let steam into the cylinders, and the train began to move off. The first mile was fairly level and, as the engine was hauling a much heavier train, their speed was limited.

"Did yer see 'oo won, Arthur?" said Jake, pointing backwards with his thumb.

"Aye, Ah think it were Fred; but 'e 'ad ter pay fer Missus 'Ighenmighty's ticket, an' she's travellin' in a diffren' carriage."

Jake chuckled, then sobered up as he glanced ahead over the boiler to see the first of the slight downhill sections of the line. He eased back the regulator, allowing the train to slow and check its momentum, and prevent its weight from pushing it out of his control. The engine itself, like very many steam engines of the day, had no brakes, and relied on the skill of the driver, the friction of the train, and the various brakemen to maintain control of the train's motion. In their three years of driving this route together, neither man had experienced any trouble, but they both knew how risky it could be if they allowed the train to travel too fast to be able to slow it when needed.

Today, the train was heavy, although no heavier than plenty of trains he had driven previously; nevertheless, Jake drove carefully, and both he and Arthur kept a vigilant eye on the track ahead. Nearing the end of their journey, dark clouds began to cover the sky, and visibility became limited. After a few minutes, the rain started. This was a problem, as the rails became slippery, and Jake had to slow the train down on the approach to the long downhill gradient where the coal siding was situated. He squinted, looking grimly for the movable sign to indicate whether the siding point was clear for them, but he couldn't quite see it.

"C'n yer see them points to the coal sidin', Arthur?" he said quickly.

Arthur stared as well. "Nae, I canna see 'em," he replied slowly and then suddenly, "Aye, ah can! They're set fer the sidin'!"

"Are yer sure?" called Jake urgently; he signalled to the brakemen, but the brakes could not hold the train, due to its weight on the wet rails. Jake set the engine into reverse, but the train's inertia forced it through the points and into the short coal siding.

"Jump, Arthur!" shouted Jake, and, as Arthur did so, the engine ran into the waiting wagons, derailing the first two and throwing lumps of coal in all directions. The labourer whose job it was to change the points and move the sign, was staring mesmerised at the oncoming train, until a plank broken from one of the wagons knocked him into the side of a nearby hut. The engine came to a stop, surrounded by broken timber and lumps of coal. Jake had held firmly onto a handrail on the footplate and was badly shaken, although not severely injured. His quick action had managed to slow the train so that the engine, tender and three carriages were derailed, leaving the remaining carriages and the loaded coal trucks on the track. But angry heads were peering out of the carriages, demanding explanations.

Arthur was lying on the ground, holding his foot, although judging from his vocabulary, the injury was not life-threatening.

"That bloody labourer 'as bin shirkin' 'is duty," he shouted. "'E needs ter pay fer this!"

But the labourer, lying by the hut where he had been thrown, did not reply: his head was at a very strange angle from his body. Jake shook his head sadly. "'E's already paid, Arthur. 'E won't be shirkin' 'is duty agin."

3 - It pays to look where you're going! (September 1853)

Jack Longbotham was standing in the Eastgate Row in Chester, watching the shoppers below while enjoying a cigar. He had quietly squirreled away two pounds over the past year, while keeping his family in the financial circumstances it was used to. His business, running three tobacconists in the city, was reasonably prosperous, and he was debating with himself whether to take that trip to Doncaster, ostensibly to look at opening a branch of the business there, but where his visit would coincide with the Doncaster Races; Jack was a betting man. His problem was that his wife also read the newspaper, and she knew of this weakness of his. *Would she realise the real purpose of his trip?*

He saw two dogs fighting below; the terrier was smaller but more aggressive than its opponent, a spaniel, which seemed to regard the smaller animal as more of a nuisance than a threat, and tried to avoid it. *A shilling on the terrier*, he thought. *If it wins, I'll go to Doncaster.* Suddenly, the terrier snapped at the spaniel's leg and drew blood, enraging the spaniel. It immediately bit back, and mangled the ear of the terrier, which ran off, yelping in pain. Jack sighed and put his shilling away. *Superstitious nonsense*, he said to himself, *I'm going anyway*.

He took a London & North Western Railway train to Manchester Victoria station, and with a short cab ride to London Road station, he connected with a Manchester, Sheffield & Lincolnshire Railway train to Doncaster. A lengthy trip, but if his two pounds were carefully invested, he might be able to make the visit very rewarding.

He wasn't the only punter heading for Doncaster. Race meetings were becoming very popular in the country, and the railway companies were making good money out of this increasing enthusiasm. They ran many race specials, finding uses for old carriages which had well passed their use-by date, so that these trains were often very long: thirty packed, old, four-wheeled carriages were common in such trains.

In London Road station that day, the M S & L (later to be proudly re-named the Great Central Railway) was having problems. There were far more passengers for Doncaster Races than they had anticipated, and the officials were scraping the barrel for carriages. The first Race Special train was so long that a second locomotive had to be found to assist it from the rear in its journey through the Pennines. The second Race Special was also very long, and set off twenty minutes later.

Jack Longbotham arrived at London Road station to find the third Race Special slowly being marshalled in the platform, and he began to search for a suitable compartment. He walked along the platform, examining the carriages, looking in vain for a comfortable first class compartment, but was unable to find one. All the carriages were old, decrepit, and not overly clean.

"What is wrong with the carriages?" he asked a porter.

"They'se nowt we c'n do about 'em, sir. They'se the on'y ones we got left." The porter was tired of questions from angry passengers.

"But I have a first class ticket!" complained Jack.

The porter smiled at him; it was nice to be able to take a toff down. "Then yer'll 'ave ter wait till termorrer, sir. They'se no more Race trains terday."

Jack set off, fuming, to try and find even a seat on the train.

The driver on the footplate was no happier than his unknown passenger; his engine, too, was one they had found semi-abandoned on a siding at the shed. It was a Sharp Roberts 2-2-2 locomotive which had been built in the early 1840s and had seen many better days. It had been retained only for emergency purposes and was no longer in daily use.

"I wonder if'n we'll ever get our train to Doncaster with this engine, Ron," growled Driver Albert Ledsham to his mate, Ron Mortimer.

"Aye," replied Ron. "When was she last run any'ow?"

"Gawd knows. Even her boiler bands are rusty. I hope she won't explode on us!"

"Can't we fail her?"

"Of course not. She hasn't refused to run yet. In any case, what d'ye think'd go on our record sheets if we did? Still, I think I'd rather put me money on a Doncaster nag than on our own steed!"

They had by this time arrived to couple up to their lengthy train. Ron looked doubtfully at it and commented, "Well, we'll know by the time we get ter the Wood'ead tunnel!" He climbed off the engine and hooked the coupling chains to their train of old four-wheelers filled with eager punters. Climbing back, he grumbled to his driver, "Too many of these old carriages fer my likin'."

Soon after, they were cleared to start, and Albert set the train gently in motion. A few miles later, passing the new Gorton Works (soon to be the flagship of the Great Central Railway), they began to feel that their earlier misgivings were possibly unjustified. Although they were still on a fairly level stretch of track, their elderly engine was showing no signs of its age; it was handling its train with relative ease.

"Wonder why they put 'er out ter grass, Bert; she seems fine ter me."

Ron was relieved: he had been expecting difficulty with the firing, but the engine was steaming satisfactorily. If he received a reply from his driver, he didn't hear it, due to the rumbling of the carriages behind.

But trouble was brewing ahead of them. The first of the three Race Specials had come to an unscheduled stop. The loaded train had simply been too heavy for the Bury-built 2-2-2 and its assisting engine. A mile or so further on, the uphill slope leading to the Woodhead tunnel, the drivers of both engines had had to stop and wait until steam could be built up, to enable them to restart the train and move through the tunnel. Even then, the train was too heavy to proceed with any speed; it only just managed to enter the tunnel, and was steaming very slowly through it. The smoke from both engines was causing distress to the passengers and crews, and it was many minutes before the front locomotive of the train exited the tunnel, to the enormous relief of its crew and passengers in the first few carriages. The train was now moving only at a walking pace, and carriages with windows had them thrown open, and passengers' heads were out, gasping for fresh air. The two men on the rear engine had been both lying on the footplate with handkerchiefs over their faces, and had not assisted with driving.

Meanwhile, the second Race Special had arrived at Dinting, just a few miles behind, where it was held by the signal bobby to warn the crew.

"Tak' it slow, lads!" he called as the train halted. "The first Race Special 'as stopped ahead, 'an they 'ad ter wait an' build up steam fer the 'ill. He then gave them the 'clear', to proceed at caution.

This they did, but as they approached the tunnel entrance, they could see the smoke still pouring out. The driver slowed then stopped the train.

"Looks like the first Special might still be in the tunnel," remarked the fireman to his mate.

"Aye, it might 'an all. You'd better check the fire and then hop out an' see if you can see 'em. I can't take the train into the tunnel, if I can't see 'em."

"Right-ho!" the fireman checked the fire, to see that it was burning satisfactorily, took a hand lamp, and walked into the tunnel. He returned five minutes later. "Yep, it's just ahead, but it's movin'. We should be safe if we take it slow. I'll stay on the front of the engine and yell out if we're getting' too close."

"Aye, but keep yer eyes well peeled!"

"I'll do that!"

The fireman climbed onto the footplate at the front, held onto the handrail, and waved his driver to go forward. The train moved off very slowly and proceeded at a snail's pace until the fireman yelled out to his driver that the first train was now visible just twenty yards ahead and moving slowly. His driver slowed the train right down until the fireman shouted, "Keep 'er at that!"

The third train had been halted at Woodhead, and was given the same warning as the second train.

"How far ahead is the second Special?" asked the driver speaking to the signal bobby.

"She left 'ere nigh on fifteen minutes back," replied the bobby, "but ye shouldn't 'ave no trouble. She were goin' well." The driver nodded and turned to his fireman. "The second is clear. She's well ahead, ses the bobby."

But the driver wasn't satisfied; his engine was shy of steam, and he wanted to get a run at the tunnel entrance, in order to reach the level stretch mid-tunnel and the downhill run beyond that.

"Build up the fire," he said, "we're going to reach the level section before we can take it easier."

Further back in the train, Jack Longbotham had found a seat, and indeed, even a congenial fellow passenger. They had been discussing horses, and were having a friendly banter as to which horse was likely to increase the weight of their purses.

"And what would you say, Mr Longbotham, to putting five shillings on 'Maiden's Worth'?"

"Maiden's Worth, Mr Earnshaw? I would say it would be simpler to just throw my five shillings out of this here window!"

"Come, come, sir; he won at Chester recently!"

"Yes, I'll grant you that, but what opposition did he have there? No, sir; my money will be on Green Emperor."

A passenger opposite them leaned over to his neighbour and whispered, "Remind me ter put me two bob on Green Emperor, Jake. I reckon this cove knows 'is 'orses." Neither Messrs Longbotham nor Earnshaw heard this, and continued their discussion with the fascinating topic moving on to other possible winners in the coming races.

On the cab, the fireman opened the firebox door, and piled more coke in. "That should do it," he said to his driver. The joint efforts of the two men seemed to pay off, as the train gathered speed on entering the tunnel; it was now travelling between twenty and twenty-five miles per hour. This was unfortunate, as the heavy weight of the train added considerably to its inertia, which meant that its stopping distance in an emergency increased greatly.

In the meantime, the first Race Special had come to a stop

just outside the tunnel exit; even with the two engines, the thirty-five old carriages had proved too much. Fortunately, the fireman on the front of the second Race Special was able to warn his driver in time for the second train to stop and avoid an accident, barely yards behind the first train.

But the relief that the enginemen in the third train had felt on reaching the tunnel, had changed to fear, as they realised they no longer had their train under control. The engine had not been fitted with brakes, and the brakemen on the old carriages found that their brakes no longer functioned with any perceptible effect. Close to the end of the tunnel, they ran headlong into the second train, killing both enginemen, as well as a number of passengers in the rear carriages of the second train. These flimsy old carriages had not been built to withstand accidents.

In Jack Longbotham's carriage, there were to be no winners that day, as everything was suddenly thrown into chaos. Passengers and their luggage were thrown around the compartment. Jack's arm was broken, and Mr Earnshaw, lying on the floor with a large bruise on his face but otherwise unhurt, stood up and brushed himself down. He assisted Jack Longbotham up, remarking; "Well now, Mr Longbotham, I think your five shillings will need to be spent on a Doctor's fee!"

Jack Longbotham did not deign to reply.

4 - First class is not always better
(April 1866)

Frederick Bassenthwaite considered himself to be a cut above most other people. Although his results at school could best be described as mediocre, his father was the village priest, and thus a pillar of the community. Young Fred believed, erroneously, that he was therefore privileged with God-given rights that other children were not entitled to. At the age of thirteen, he was apprenticed to a local engineering firm, and his confident manner soon had him promoted to a senior position, with a salary which later allowed him to choose a young wife who was easily browbeaten. Still in his late twenties, his arrogance was not tempered by the public revelation that his father had been using his churchly duties to introduce young boys in matters which had nothing at all to do with religious teachings. The church hurried its priest away to a distant parish, and in the village pub the younger Bassenthwaite consistently claimed a lofty ignorance of his father's activities.

Once he had qualified as an engineer (a quiet sovereign slipped to a responsible overseer had been of some assistance here), he sought employment with the London & South Western Railway, in their track maintenance section. Here too, his assertive manner among his peers assisted in his promotion, and, at a relatively young age, he was made the foreman of a track repair gang based in Basingstoke. He was even given a railway house at a very reasonable rent. But Foreman Bassenthwaite was not averse to cutting the occasional corner in his quest to be known as a man who could 'get things done'. Consequently, his gang were often employed on the more responsible and tricky jobs, with senior management focusing on the outcomes and turning a 'blind eye' to safe working, such as it was in those days.

On a pleasant April morning, the gang was busy relaying the trackwork on a curve in a cutting before a low viaduct on the Plymouth to London main line. Fred had the timetable with him, and had checked that they now had over an hour until the next up train to Waterloo was due.

"Right-ho lads, get this rail out and let's have the replacement rail in place, then we can let the first boat train through slowly; and when that's gone, we can deal with the second rail."

The gangers seized their tools, and began to lever out and remove the old rail bolts that were holding the rail in place. One of the gangers looked up along the track and saw the flagman.

"Mr Bassenthwaite, sir, is the flagman far enough away? I thought he was supposed to be a thousand yards back from us."

Fred glared at the man. "Are you trying to tell me how to do my job?" he snapped angrily.

"Oh no, of course not, sir. I was just thinking—"

"You're not paid to think, you cheeky young devil; that's my job. You're just paid to do what you're bid!"

"Yessir!" and the ganger picked up his crowbar and bent to the offending rail.

At Southampton dock terminus, three boat trains were marshalled ready to bring the transatlantic passengers to London. They were waiting for an American ship to arrive and unload its passengers and mail. Its captain was waiting outside the harbour for the weather to moderate and allow his ship to dock. It was another hour before he could do so; this meant that the first boat train would be an hour and a half behind schedule. This train had a new Falcon class 2-4-0 express engine to haul it, and was mainly for the well-heeled passengers, with five first-class carriages, one second-class carriage, two passenger luggage vans, and a full brake van for the large amount of luggage, all necessary for the comfort of such passengers.

Driver Arnold Goldman looked down the platform at the porters eagerly awaiting tips from wealthy passengers and remarked to his fireman Jimmy Butterworth, "There could be ructions soon, Jimmy; some of the passengers'll be wanting to get to London in a hurry, and if the porters don't get them good seats, you might hear a spot o' language!"

His fireman smiled: "I don't think I'll hear anything I haven't already heard, Arnold. I served two years in the Crimean War!"

Arnold laughed, "Oh aye, I forgot about that!"

Soon, the first passengers could be seen hurrying onto the platform, porters struggling with their heavy luggage. Yet among them was one person who was clearly in no hurry; he was accompanied by three policemen and four porters. Everyone else gave way before him, and his porters took him to a reserved compartment; here he took his time carefully mounting the prepared steps as the carriage door was held open for him.

"A very important cove!" commented Arnold. "I wonder who he is?" There was no reply from Jimmy, who was checking the condition of the fire. In fact, the passenger had been a senior Confederate government official. He was seeking to re-establish his fortune by contacting his pre-war British business clients, and was complaining to one of them with him in the train. "Our Northerners have no damn sense," he declared, "they cannot see that using slaves makes our trade very reasonable. You Britishers are going to have to pay higher prices for our tobacco and cigars." He shook his head, grumbling, "Somebody should have dealt with Abe Lincoln before he became President."

The remaining passengers were now boarding the train without the usual struggling with luggage and pushing and shoving normally associated with crowds boarding trains. These wealthy patrons could hire porters to do the undignified work of procuring suitable accommodation for them. In the only second-class carriage, one elderly lady berated her husband; "Why can't you make enough money for us to travel like that, Jeremiah Witherspoon?" she gazed in envy at a stately lady marching past, with a porter in tow, who was struggling with her three large cases.

"I've done me best, Gladys;" he replied. "Just remember our first train trip when we 'ad to travel third class!" She sniffed in indignation but did not deign to reply. Finally, almost seventy-five minutes late, the train was permitted to leave.

"We've got a lot of time to catch up on, Jimmy," said Arnold to his fireman, "I hope you've had a good plateful of porridge this morning to build up your muscles."

"We could be in trouble then, Arnold," laughed Jimmy. "I might be knackered by the time we reach Eastleigh, and you'll have to take over!"

Both men laughed; it was no secret between them that Jimmy was a far better fireman than Arnold had ever been. Jimmy had a solid build, and was never seriously troubled by long journeys. They raced past Eastleigh, and were soon passing Winchester, having already picked up seven minutes.

Back at Southampton dock, the word had been telegraphed through that the first boat train was running seventy minutes late, and a runner was sent to the track-laying gang with word of the delay in the boat train express, plus a warning that it would be passing at full speed. Young George Betts, an apprentice ganger, approached Fred Bassenthwaite with apprehension; he knew of the man's dislike of him. George had good reason: he had once been instructed to fetch Fred's lunch box. He had done so, and placed the box conveniently on a flat truck right at Fred's left hand. But the flat truck had been in a passing freight which had been stopped at the signals and then, once the signal was cleared, moved on, taking Fred's lunch with it.

"What the hell do you want, Betts?" demanded Fred angrily.

"Message from Woking yard, sir. It's important."

"I'll decide what's important, you impudent young dog! Now, put it there and clear off before you get my boot."

"Yessir." George put the paper on the toolbox as Fred indicated and scurried off before he felt Mr Bassenthwaite's footwear.

"Cheeky young bugger," muttered Fred to himself and without looking at it, put the paper into his pocket.

Some time later, he pulled his watch out of his waistcoat pocket and checked the time. The replacement rail had been fitted, and was firmly in place. They were now waiting for the first train to pass. Fred suddenly remembered the message, and dug it out of his pocket.

"Right lads," he said, "the first boat train is running seventy minutes late. We can get that second rail replaced well before it gets here, so she'll have a clear run through. Now get busy."

The second thirty-foot length of rail was quickly removed and placed to one side, and the six gangers lifted the new rail into position.

Along the main up line, all the signal bobbies, knowing the

importance of first boat train with its valued passengers, had been careful to avoid any possible delay to its run. Less important passenger trains and all scheduled freight trains were held up until the boat train had passed. The result for Jimmy and Arnold had been a dream run; they had been able to pick up almost half an hour. The engine was an acknowledged racehorse, the signals were in their favour, and the coke was of top quality. They were speeding along at a steady seventy miles an hour but, as usual, Arnold reduced the speed to about fifty miles per hour as they approached the viaduct, leading to the curve, where Fred Bassenthwaite's gang was working.

But rounding the curve, Jimmy happened to be watching the track ahead and saw the flagman and then the gangers, only a couple of hundred yards ahead of him.

"Men on the line, Arnold!" he shouted urgently.

Arnold glanced ahead, swore, and lowered the regulator as much as he dared, in a vain attempt to slow the train. But the flagman was far too close to his gang, and the train ran onto the viaduct; it rounded the curve, reached the section with the loose rail, and the engine derailed instantly and crashed onto its side. Nearly all of the carriages derailed and the first three of them following the engine also tipped over, severely damaging their wooden sides. Only the last four carriages remained upright, but off the rails. The shocked gangers rushed over to assist the injured passengers trying to scramble out of their ruptured compartments. Fortunately over the next half-hour, two doctors among the passengers were able to give immediate first aid to the injured passengers and to both crewmen; they were also able to confirm the deaths of five passengers.

By the time more help arrived, with carts and horses able to take the more severely wounded for hospital attention, most of the passengers were out of the train on the track, either helping, or being assisted. Only passengers in the last two carriages were without serious injuries, including Mr Witherspoon, who had left his carriage and hurried to see what he could do to help. Later, he returned to his worried wife waiting in their compartment; his coat was torn and there was, his wife believed, a large patch of blood on his trousers. She was torn between relief at seeing him unharmed and the need to remonstrate with him about the state of his clothing, when he said, "There, Gladys me love, see what 'appens, when yer travel in the first class." With tears in her eyes, she simply hugged him, and held her peace.

At the subsequent inquiry, Foreman Bassenthwaite was found responsible for the accident. He had not allowed sufficient time for the boat train to pass through, and had failed to follow correct safety procedure; further, he had not positioned his flagman the stipulated distance away, nor had he had detonators placed in position for any oncoming train to be able to stop in time. He was fined, dismissed from his job, and turned out of his house. Driver Goldman and Fireman Butterworth were released from hospital after two weeks and returned to their jobs; no failing on their part was recorded.

5 - A hazardous run to Berlin (January 1872)

Fireman Heinz Waller shook the snow off his boots as he neared the locomotive shed of the Hamburg-Berlin Railway Company at Hamburg's Berliner Station. It had been snowing hard for several days now, and he was not looking forward to his next duty, which was to fire his locomotive on the Berlin express, due out in ninety minutes. He fervently hoped that the shed staff had coaled the engine with decent coal; they'd had had some awful stuff recently, which had not made his job easier. He and his driver, Werner Herrman, had striven hard to keep their locomotive moving with a local train to Bergedorf five days earlier, and the relief crew had had to fail the engine on its return to Hamburg. There had been a great deal of fuss in the shed and the coal supplier had been threatened with loss of contract if he sold more of the same to the company. His so-called 'steam coal' had been mixed with inferior coal, and the engines (and consequently the enginemen) had suffered; late trains damaged the company's reputation, and financial loss could occur. Shareholders took a very dim view of this state of affairs.

"Well, Heinz, all fine with the family?" Werner's cheery greeting was welcome on such a day. He was already in the cab of their Borsig-built 2-4-0 express locomotive.

"Mornin' Werner," Heinz returned the greeting with some optimism; Werner would not have been so cheerful, if he had detected something wrong with their locomotive. Werner was in his fifties with a heavy build and a normally happy disposition, which endeared him to his colleagues. He was an excellent driver, and knew his engines extremely well. He always gave help to his fireman, and he seemed to have a special relationship with Heinz, for which the latter was very thankful. "What sort of coal have we got today?" asked Heinz glancing, into the tender.

"Seems satisfactory," replied Werner, "at least on top, but when we're well on the way, we may find different underneath."

"Like we struggled last week?"

"If we go through that again on an express, the foreman will get a lengthy earful from me, and we could change coal suppliers."

Heinz laughed, although he was well aware that Werner was serious, and his words had weight in the shed. The fireman checked the fire, shovelling a little more coal into a low spot, and, after checking the gauges for steam pressure and water level, nodded to his mate that all was well. He placed his lunch bag on a shelf in the tender, next to his bottle of beer; he favoured sandwiches made with his favourite black bread with Leberkäse, whereas Werner preferred grey bread with Mettwurst if the butcher had any. One of Heinz's habits once a month was to visit the large delicatessen in the city, and marvel at the range of Wurst on sale. Last week, the sales assistant had told him proudly that they had 147 varieties. Staring at their range, he could believe it.

"Ready to move off, are we Heinz?" Werner brought his daydreaming to an abrupt end, and they moved off-shed to wait at the starter signal. Out of their shed, they felt the snow falling harder, and Heinz took his coffee and placed it nearer the firebox, to prevent it from freezing during the run. The protection of their cab was dependent upon the direction of the wind. An easterly was a little to be preferred, in that the front of the cab and the roof would protect them from the worst. Side winds were unpleasant, because the side plates on their engine only went to waist height. A wind from the north-west was another matter altogether; it would send snow right over the low tender and straight into their backs in the cab. "We're lucky today, Werner," remarked Heinz, "we've an easterly."

"Yeah," replied Werner, "direct from Siberia."

They pulled into Hamburg's Berliner Station, and backed onto their train, where Heinz dropped down to the low platform and hurried to couple up the engine to the train. He climbed back into the cab and readied the fire for the initial run to Bergedorf, their first stop. The train with its dozen coaches was full, with passengers hurrying to choose their seats and carrying their luggage, or with their porters guiding them to the better seats.

First class passengers were offered hot bricks wrapped in cloth for their feet. These could be exchanged at stations along the line during the journey for freshly-heated bricks. Passengers in the second- and third-classes had to content themselves with sitting as closely as they could to the carriages' stoves, with heavy fur coats and bottles of schnapps to keep them warm.

For railwaymen, the matter was less straightforward. Point-blades and crossings often froze, snow obscured the signals, shunters were unable to see details of the trains they were dealing with, and enginemen were often on engines with very little protection from the weather. But by far the worst off were the conductor-brakemen on the long-distance trains; every third carriage had a small seat high outside at the end of the carriage, upon which they perched. Their job was to check the tickets of the boarding passengers, and then to climb up to the seat to be able to apply the brakes at a signal from the driver. They would assist in slowing the train on approaching a stop. In cold weather, these men had to sit wrapped up in heavy coats for hours on end to keep an eye on their section of the train and respond to the directions of the driver. There had been talk of building a small hut up there for the convenience of the brakemen, but so far little had been done.

"All aboard!" came the cry from the stationmaster, the signal showed clear, and Werner lifted the regulator gently as the locomotive felt its load and began to move off smoothly. The first stretch was an easy run, without any significant gradients, and it gave the two crewmen a good idea of the condition of their engine.

"You know I feel really sorry for those brakemen," said Heinz to Werner, "the poor buggers are stuck up there in the wind and snow, and I often wonder how they cope. Weather like this is bad enough for us in the cab, but it must be a nightmare for them."

Werner glanced back along the train. "Aye, but I bet they've each got a bottle of schnapps up in the pocket with 'em."

"Can't really blame 'em for that," replied Heinz, "I can keep shovellin' to keep warm; all they can do is to sit up there freezin' on their arses and takin' a quick nip now and again."

"And get sacked, if they're caught nipping," added Werner.

"It's no life for a railwayman."

"Especially not in winter with the wind from the Baltic," added Werner.

But the weather in Bergedorf was no better. In fact it was getting worse. The wind had picked up, and snow flurries were being driven horizontally; visibility was reduced to only a couple of hundred metres, as the train moved off once more. "This is not going to be one of our better trips, Heinz," said Werner, leaning out of the cab and trying to stare ahead through the snow. "I can't see the signals too well. We may have to slow down which our relief in Wittenberg won't like at all."

"The passengers won't be too happy, either."

"They'll have to lump it. We don't control the weather."

Indeed, the snow was thickening fast, and the cold was getting bitter. They were travelling through the open country of the North German plain, and they saw nobody on the platforms of the small country stations they passed slowly through; only an occasional lamp glimpsed through a window. Farms could sometimes be seen, if they were close to the railway, but they too were only vague outlines in the driving snow. The stop at Schwarzenbek, the junction for the Bad Oldesloe branch, gave the two enginemen welcome but only momentary relief to rub their eyes and warm their hands at the firebox, while passengers left and boarded the train, assisted by the few porters, before the stationmaster gave them the signal to leave.

Both Werner and Heinz knew the route well, and could judge roughly where signals could be expected, but by the time they had reached Brahlstorf, their eyes were getting tired and sore from having to slow to see the signals, and they were thirty-five minutes down.

"We're going to have to try and make up some time before Ludwigslust, if possible, Heinz," grumbled Werner, as they steamed out of the station.

"Not going to be easy, if we have to slow down at each signal post, Werner," replied Heinz, "and I heard Driver Henkelthein last week saying he had seen a small pack of wolves as they passed Grabow."

Werner nodded. "I heard that too, and Hinkelthein's a reliable cove; he doesn't lie."

Ten minutes after leaving Brahlstorf, the snow had become too thick to see more than 100 metres, and they had to slow the train further in order to catch sight of the next signal; it showed clear, but when Werner raised the regulator to increase speed, the wheels slipped. He lowered the regulator and tried again, but had the same result. After a third try without success, he shook his head. "Sorry Heinz, you'll have to nip down and shovel some loose ballast under the driving wheels. I'll keep a sharp eye out for any unwelcome wolf."

Heinz grabbed a shovel, climbed down to the track, and began to shovel ballast onto the rails in front of the moving wheels, as Werner gingerly increased the speed, and the wheels began to grip as they ground the stones on the rails. The slow process continued for a few metres, until Werner called out "I think I've got her, Heinz!" Heinz climbed quickly back on to the cab as the train gradually picked up speed. By the time they arrived in Ludwigslust, they were forty-four minutes down, with another forty-odd kilometres to run. The weather seemed colder than ever as they ran towards Wittenberg, but the enginemen were glad to see the station lights in the distance. On approaching the station throat, Werner found that his speed was still rather more than he wanted. "I think the brakemen are a little slow, Heinz," he said, "they should be applying their brakes by now." But he was able to bring their train to a standstill at the station, and it was with a real sense of relief that they entered Wittenberg Station.

Heinz climbed down to uncouple their locomotive as the relieving engine, waiting on the adjacent track, began to move forward to the points, to be able to back onto their train once Werner had taken their engine clear. But Heinz seemed to be held up by something; he didn't return to the cab straightaway.

Werner saw two medical attendants hurrying along the platform. "Sick passenger", he said to himself, as he waited for his fireman to return. Then he saw more attendants rushing along the platform, carrying stretchers. He looked along the train to see a brakeman being assisted down from his seat to the platform. "Get the poor bugger into the warmth quick before he freezes to death," he muttered, as Heinz climbed back into the cab. He was shaking.

"Open the firebox, lad, you're still shivering."

"Yeah." The reply was automatic, as if Heinz hadn't properly listened.

"I saw one of the brakemen being helped down. Is he being looked after?"

"Yeah, now we need two replacement brakemen."

"Two? Why two?"

"The second is dead."

6 - An old dog knows best
(March 1885)

In the 1880s, Wolverhampton Works at Stafford Road was the second largest Great Western workshop after Swindon, and concentrated on the standard gauge locomotives of the company's network, while Swindon was engaged with the broad gauge rolling stock. Aside from building new engines, Wolverhampton Works also maintained engines from some of the smaller companies which had been bought out by the GWR; the Shrewsbury & Chester, and the Shrewsbury & Birmingham railways included. Some of these older engines were well past their prime, and many had to be scrapped.

Foreman Daniel Southwick stared at the workman in front of him. "How the hell did the GWR manage to recruit you to this responsible job?" he asked sarcastically. "You've got no notion as to what you're supposed to be doing!"

The foreman was standing by the huge lathe in the wheel assembly workshop. Elderly fitter Eli Cohen was checking the axle of a pair of driving wheels from an 0-4-2 ex-Shrewsbury & Birmingham Railway locomotive built in 1849 by Stephensons. Eli had found a hairline crack, probably due to a manufacturing fault, and he had claimed the axle should be discarded, but his foreman disagreed. "Why should the company throw good money away simply on the word of a lowly fitter?" he grunted. "That axle is fine, and will not be replaced. Now get on with your work, and don't bother me with such piddling matters." He walked away, muttering about daft old codgers who should have been retired before they became senile. Foreman Southwick had been promoted recently, and felt that he should make his position clear to all his fitters, and Fitter Cohen hadn't shown him the deference he believed was appropriate.

Eli scratched his head. He knew that a tiny hairline crack was a serious danger sign, and was pondering whether to go over his boss's head to a more senior supervisor. If an accident occurred, he knew who would get the blame. He decided to write a note to the foreman, to cover himself in case the foreman should deny any later responsibility.

Two days later, Foreman Southwick came back to him with the letter to him in his hand. He was furious. "I told you to forget this nonsense!" he shouted. "If you ignore my instructions once more, I'll have you dismissed." Eli shrugged; he had done his duty and it had been thrown back at him.

After other minor repairs, the locomotive was sent back to its home shed in Chester, where it was to finish its days on the local West Kirby route in the Wirral.

Driver Jim Benson of Chester GWR shed checked the roster board and walked out to where the 0-4-2 ex-S & B R locomotive was waiting for his attention. Fireman Dick Allanson was standing next to the cab step, with one foot on it.

"Going to actually get on the engine then, Dick?" laughed Jim. 'There's work to be done." He liked to tease his fireman on occasions; the repartee was diverting. Dick looked up from the boot he was cleaning and grinned, waving the disgusting-looking stick that he was wiping his boot with. "Happy to do so, Jim, if you're happy to have horse shit on your cab floor."

"You what?"

"I got off the tram outside the station this morning and stepped right into a little souvenir which the tram horse left."

"You bring horse shit onto my cab and I'll hose you down with the coal watering pipe!"

"Come off it! You can see I'm cleaning my boot."

"Well I hope you keep a better eye on the signals on our run to West Kirby this morning than you do at getting off the tram."

Dick grinned, finished cleaning his boot, and climbed aboard to turn his attention to the fire. The men had another forty-five minutes before they needed to take their engine out of the shed area and pick up their train, but they were competent men, and familiar with the engine still fresh from its overhaul. While Dick prepared the fire and checked the water level and steam pressure, Jim walked around the engine, oiling the points, and then filling in the details of the engine's condition in his notebook.

"Have we time for a quick brew?" Fireman Allanson had a permanent thirst for a brew of tea, and Jim Benson often wondered how his mate could keep it all inside him on longer trips. Jim himself was always careful to take tea only when there was a prospect of a nearby WC to relieve himself after a drink.

"Worried about your g.s.b.?" asked Dick. "We've still got fifteen minutes."

"G.s.b.?" queried Jim.

"Gill-sized bladder," explained Dick.

Jim chuckled. "No, I hadn't heard that expression, but it's certainly accurate. I sometimes feel like a piss when I only even *think* of having a mug of tea." He pulled the big watch out of his waistcoat and looked at it. "Yes, we'll risk it; there's a bog in the canteen on the platform."

By the time Jim had finished his sentence, Dick had the shovel out and in the firebox, with the billycan on it. The two mugs were on the shelf ready above the fire-hole. In a few seconds, the billycan was withdrawn from the fire, four heaped spoonfuls of tea were dropped in, and the billy was swung round to mix the brew.

I don't know how he does it, thought Jim, as he watched his mate. Milk and sugar went in, and the mugs of tea were ready to drink within a minute of the question being asked. *And I bet he had three cups with his breakfast just over an hour ago!*

Dick put his empty mug down and smacked his lips. "Ahh, that's better," he said. "I only had time for three cups this morning."

Jim shook his head in amusement, as the shed signal dropped for them to leave the shed and move on to Platform Three. They backed onto the seven six-wheel coaches, and Dick climbed down to couple up. As soon as he returned, Jim slipped into the railwaymen's toilet in the nearby canteen.

Once they had the signal and the wave of the guard's green flag, they moved off and eased gently over to the right at the station throat and onto the main line to Birkenhead and out of the city, with the engine running easily.

Dick paused in his shovelling coal into the firebox and remarked, "She's running nicely, Jim. I think this old girl enjoyed the overhaul at Wolverhampton."

Jim nodded. "You're right, Dick, they've done a good job on her; we'll know for sure once she tackles those points south of Hooton onto the West Kirby line. I don't know why the PW gangers don't get 'em fixed. Enginemen have been complaining for years about them." Permanent Way gangers were responsible for the maintenance of the trackwork.

They paused at the first stop at Upton-by-Chester for three people to board the train, and then once more at the village of Mollington for another ten to board. The stop at Hooton was longer; the engine had to be uncoupled and run round the train, because the line to West Kirby left from the south end of the station, forcing through trains from Chester to reverse direction. This also meant that tender engines had to travel tender first from Hooton to West Kirby; but tenders were generally low enough for the crew to have a satisfactory view of the line ahead.

Jim took the train gingerly over the poorly-laid points, but their locomotive took them without complaint.

"We're in luck, Dick," said Jim, as they headed towards Neston, "She's in good nick." Dick grunted as he shovelled coal into the back ends of the firebox; enough to take them well past Parkgate, the stop at which he hoped they could have another quick brew. But he was to be disappointed; at Parkgate they were occupied helping an elderly and querulous passenger into the train.

"Awkward old sod!" muttered Dick as they got away ten minutes late. Jim's eyes twinkled, "Give him a break, Dick," he remarked, "Just remember you'll be an awkward old sod too, when you're eighty."

They were able to make up time, and arrived at West Kirby dead on time. Dick uncoupled the engine from the coaches, and Jim moved her forward and over the points to reverse past the train and re-couple ready for the return run, for which they have to wait an hour.

"Now you can have that gallon of tea you've been thirsting for," said Jim with a grin. Dick just grunted, but again, had the can in the boiler before Jim had finished speaking.

As they were leaving West Kirby for Chester, however, Jim was uneasy. The engine seemed a little unsteady, and even Dick noticed it while he was using the pricker to even up the coal layer in the firebox. He looked up at his driver.

"Something wrong, Jim?" he asked.

"Not sure. Something's not right," Jim replied. Suddenly the engine lurched to the right, derailed, and came to a sudden stop, leaning over. Fortunately, they had not been travelling fast, and the tender and coaches stayed on the track, although the sudden stop injured a few passengers.

Dick on the right-hand side of the cab, saw the front driving wheel splayed out under the locomotive, and the coupling rod was bent out of shape. "Jim, the bloody front driver's come off the axle, or the axle's broken!" he called.

The injured passengers were in luck: a doctor was on the train, and he examined them and decided that none needed to go to hospital. The engine was a very different matter: the leading driving wheel axle had fractured. At West Kirby, fortunately, a spare engine was available to take over the train to Chester, where the damaged engine was also taken later. The broken axle was sent to Wolverhampton for examination, while the damaged engine had its axle replaced.

Driver Benson spoke severely to his fireman as they were taken back to Chester shed: "It was that gallon of tea you drank, Dick; that's what broke the axle."

"Yes, it must have been, Jim, I didn't have time for a piss afterwards." They chuckled to cover their mutual fright.

In the workshop, Foreman Daniel Southwick was summoned to appear before Mr Cameron, the departmental manager. "You allowed an axle with a hairline crack to leave the workshop, Daniel. Why?"

"I trusted the fitter concerned, sir. He's been with us for many years, and I assumed he would have seen it."

"He didn't mention it to you at all?"

"No sir, he did not. Had he done so, I would have checked it myself."

"You are quite sure about that?"

"Yessir. Quite sure."

"Are you aware that before you were appointed to your present position, the job was offered to Fitter Cohen?"

Daniel Southwick was startled; he had had no idea. "No sir, I was not aware of that."

"Eli Cohen is the best fitter in the department; he knows what he is doing. But he didn't want the job; he said he was happy where he was. He claims he even informed you in writing of his view."

"That's nonsense, sir. He did no such thing."

"You destroyed his letter quickly, did you?"

"Yes, I burnt.. I - er; no, of course not. How could I, sir? I never received it."

The manager reached for a sheet of paper on his desk and wrote on it for a few moments and put it into an envelope. He looked up at Daniel grimly. "I trusted you, Daniel," he said, "but I know you received a letter from Eli. He sent one to me as well, but I assumed you had dealt with the matter." He gave the envelope to Foreman Southwick. "That's your dismissal notice. I want you out of here by lunchtime today."

As Daniel left, he heard the manager call an office boy, saying, "Find Eli Cohen and tell him I want to see him in ten minutes."

7 - A fumble on the Furness
(April 1906)

It was raining heavily at the busy station at Whitehaven on the Furness Railway, where an express for Barrow was waiting for the connection from Carlisle to arrive. In the engine's cab were Driver George Sturgess and his young mate Fireman Eric Giles. George was a tall man in his middle fifties, with a wealth of driving experience, whereas Eric, in his late twenties was, like many young firemen, convinced that he already knew as much about driving as his driver. George was well aware of Eric's opinion, and was both tolerant and good-natured enough about it; furthermore, he liked his young colleague. He was, on the other hand, looking forward patiently to (and expecting to be entertained by) Eric's discovery of his mistaken opinion.

Their locomotive was one of the Pettigrew K3 4-4-0s, a tried and proven class of engine. They were known to be fairly reliable and, with their six-foot driving wheels, suitable for the Furness expresses, although rumours were about that Mr Pettigrew was working on a more powerful design because the expresses were getting heavier. Fifteen minutes late, the Maryport & Carlisle connecting train from Maryport arrived, and passengers for the Furness train were quickly chivvied from it and onto the waiting Barrow express.

"We're off, Eric lad," said George. "It's next stop Sellafield Junction, an' we might 'ave our tea break at Ravenglass by 'la'al Rattie'." 'La'al Rattie' was what the locals called the three-foot narrow gauge Ravenglass & Eskdale Railway, which was used mainly to transport iron ore from the mines near the village of Boot down Eskdale to the coast. Passenger trains were provided, but they were unpopular with the management because they did not bring in sufficient profit. The line had been experiencing decreasing traffic in recent years, and its stock needed more maintenance than it was getting.

"Aal reet, Mr S," replied Eric as he checked the gauges and opened the firebox to check the fire. All seemed in order because he was a careful young man and had checked the fire conscientiously while they were waiting for the connection from Carlisle.

For George, the route south along the coast was always a pleasure; he loved the scenery, with the steep hills on the left and the coastal views on the right, especially past St Bees. He glanced from time to time approvingly as his fireman fastidiously attended to his duties, keeping the fire at the correct state to provide the necessary steam and watching the pressure gauges. He had once wondered why Eric had always checked the steam and fire thoroughly before they passed through stations, and had concluded that it was because the lad wanted time free to keep an eye out for any young ladies as they passed. He fully sympathized with the youngster's interest; George himself had once been called a 'randy young devil' by his own driver who had caught him chatting up the girl who later became his wife.

The run down to Ravenglass was uneventful, and the brew at Ravenglass had been very welcome, but their departure was held up. The heavy rain up the valley of the River Esk had delayed the narrow gauge train from Boot; the driver of the poorly maintained engine had been forced to slow the speed of his train in order to ensure that the brakes had a chance to grip on the wet and greasy rails.

As the few passengers transferred from the narrow gauge train, Eric caught sight of long blonde locks down the back of a lady. He leaned out of the cab in the hope that she would turn round and give him a frontal view. She did, and he was immediately impressed; she was beautiful, and he wondered how he might find an excuse to get into conversation with her. He kept a sharp eye out every time they stopped, but she stayed out of sight and only appeared again when they pulled into Barrow. Here, Eric was frustrated once more; he had to descend to rail level to uncouple the engine from their coaches, and by the time he climbed back up, he could see the blonde locks disappearing way down the platform.

As Eric climbed back into the cab, George said with a grin, "You missed summat special, young feller; a very attractive young lady got off while you were busy down on the track.

You'd've have liked her!"

Eric grinned back, "Nae, Mr S," he replied, "I di'n't miss 'er. I watched 'er as she got on at Ravenglass; she came off t'Ratty." He privately determined to see if she returned that day, and kept an eye open when they reached Ravenglass again on the return run. Three days later, he saw her again as she boarded their Whitehaven train at Barrow. *Hmm*, he thought to himself, *I might see if I can 'ave a word or two when we stop at Ravenglass where she might gerroff the train.*

A few minutes before reaching Ravenglass, George remarked on the need for a brew at the next stop. Eric agreed and began fishing out his tea and a sandwich ready for when they pulled up. As they halted, he looked out of the cab, saw the girl descending from her coach, and called over his shoulder, "I'll just pop out for a minute, Mr S." He dropped to the platform, and strolled up to the girl.

"Everything alright for you, miss?" he asked.

She looked at this young man in surprise. "Oh yes," she replied, "I'm catching the Ratty back home to Boot, where I live."

"I'm told it is very beautiful up there in t'hills," said Eric quickly trying to improve his speech.

"Indeed it is," she responded. "You should come up one day."

This sounded almost like an invitation, and Eric was quick to take advantage of it. "Well, I'm free nex' weekend, I might pop up then," he said.

The girl smiled at him. "There's a little tea-shop in the village;" she said. "I usually have a cup there on Saturdays at about four of the clock."

Sounds like an invitation, thought Eric, and said, "I'll be there and looking forward to it."

Back in the cab, George shook his head sadly. "You missed your tea, Eric; we're off again in half a minute."

"'S all reet, Mr S; I've a date on the weekend with a young lady!"

"That blonde girl?"

"Aye, that's 'er!" Eric's grin spoke volumes and George smiled, remembering his own courting days.

Eric found waiting for the Saturday something of a trial, and when the day finally arrived, he was able to save the fare from Barrow by offering to fire on a coal train of empties as far as Ravenglass. Once in the village of Boot, he found the tea-shop and sat down there at four o'clock exactly. The girl arrived a few minutes later, and was pleased to see a spruced-up Eric. They chatted and drank their tea, but Eric was surprised to note that, when walking through the village, none of the young men gave the girl – her name was Sandra, she told him - a second glance. This puzzled him; in Barrow, every lad in town would have ogled her, and envied him. He was not to know that in the village she was well-known as a tease. She had egged on every lad in the village, yet not a single one of them, in spite of determined efforts, had ever got as far as a stolen kiss.

On his next duty, George asked Eric how he had got on with the young lady. Eric smirked and told George that Sandra had promised to meet him in a few days' time in Barrow. He asked if he could show her where he worked.

Driver Sturgess was surprised at the question. "Of course, lad," he said, "We're on the Carnforth run next week. She won't be the only passenger on the platform. You know yourself that people often come to chat while we're waiting for the 'off'."

"Err- I was 'opin' I might be able to show 'er the cab, like," said Eric hesitantly.

"Bring her into the cab?" George was astonished, "Don't be daft, lad. You know you could lose your job for that." He frowned. "So could I for that matter, if I allowed it."

"Oh yeah. Sorry Mr S."

They had a surprise when they backed into the station to pick up their Carnforth train the following Monday. Malcolm Kershaw, one of the platform inspectors, was waiting for them, and their train had a set of freshly painted blue coaches with white upper panels. It looked extremely smart behind their clean Indian-red express engine.

"Morning lads," called out Mr Kershaw with a grin, as he climbed into the cab. "You've been given a clean rake of coaches fresh out of the paint shop; and I've been told to tell you not to damage them!"

"Now then, Mr Kershaw," said George laughing, "why on earth would we do that to such a fine train?"

The two men chatted while they were waiting; they had twenty minutes until the departure of the train.

"I'll just go an' check t'coupling agen, Mr S," muttered Eric to George, and he slipped down from the cab.

"You've got a keen young lad there, George," commented Mr Kershaw.

"Aye, he's good lad most of the time." replied George.

But Eric had seen what he had hoped for: Sandra was walking along the platform. He had informed her which train he would be on when she had told him she would be in Barrow that day. He had told her he would be back on the return train at five in the evening and if she was still in Barrow, they could go for a meal.

Punctually at five, they were back in Barrow station, and Eric dropped to the track to uncouple the vacuum brake and couplings and, as he mounted the platform again, he caught sight of Sandra walking towards him.

At that moment, however, George called him from the cab. "Quickly, Eric, come on up;" he said climbing down. "I've got to have a word with Mr Kershaw, the platform inspector. I forgot to mention something this morning."

Eric climbed into the cab, watching while his driver walked to a nearby office, and then signalled Sandra to climb into the cab with him. She did so, gingerly holding her dress so that it didn't brush against anything grimy. In the meantime, a tank engine coupled up to the other end of the coaches and drew them slowly away to the coach sidings, while the platform emptied of passengers.

Sandra gazed around the cab, saying, "So this is where you work, Eric. It seems complicated. What's this lever for?" She took hold of the regulator.

"Don't touch that!" shouted Eric in a panic. He had noticed that the engine brake was not on.

"Oh, sorry!" Sandra took her hand swiftly off the lever. She apologised so prettily that Eric was suddenly overcome with passion. He seized her shoulders to give her a kiss, but she turned her face away with an indignant "No!"

Eric ignored her, and tried again to grab her, but she ducked out of his way and, in reaching forward, he lost his balance and caught the regulator instead of her shoulder. His seizure of the regulator caused the engine to move forward a few yards before he could apply the brake to stop it. Sandra hurriedly left the cab as the engine began to glide forward, and Eric, desperately grabbing the regulator, brought it down, applied the engine brake and the engine came slowly to a stop.

Driver Sturgess appeared from the office a few minutes later, and stared at the locomotive in disbelief. He climbed into the cab to see his fireman sitting on the fireman's seat, eating a sandwich.

"I could've bloody sworn I left us further back." he stated, "You haven't moved her, have you?"

"Me, Mr S? Why would I move 'er?" Eric was all innocence.

On his walk home, Eric was very thoughtful: *Reet 'orrible day, that were. Lost me girl an' almost lost me job, an' aal! I'll 'ave to learn ter keep me 'an's ter meself in t'cab!*

8 - A handy tunnel
(November 1916)

Michael Timson had been working on the North Eastern Railway for several years, first as a handyman about the NER shed at Berwick, and, early in 1897, had been promoted to Cleaner. He knew that sooner or later he would be able to advance himself, initially to Fireman, and eventually to Driver. This had been his ambition ever since he was toddler. His parents had long accepted this, and had given him what encouragement they could. He had joined the NER in 1893, at the age of 14, and had been employed on a range of minor duties, until the shed's foreman had decided he was sufficiently reliable to be installed in a cleaning gang. Here, he could clean not only engines of the NER with their light green paintwork, but also sometimes those of the North British Railway, whose dark, mustard-coloured engines terminated at Berwick for their southern expresses to be handed over to North Eastern crews for Newcastle, York and London. By 1904, he was a fireman, and worked on the local services to Sprouston and Coldstream. In 1908, he was transferred to Carlisle, where he got to meet enginemen from other railways: the Glasgow & South Western, the Midland, the London & North Western and the little Maryport & Carlisle railways.

He was really enjoying his work when, in August of that year, Britain and its Empire declared war on Germany. Driver Timson had a peaceful and quiet and disposition; he was by no means an aggressive man, and the thought of going to fight, shoot at, or stab a bayonet into, another man was totally abhorrent to him. Yet many of his railway colleagues signed up eagerly for the armed forces, seeking the assumed glory promised them by the recruiting officers. This put him into a difficult position: on the one hand, he felt the pressure of both patriotism and a reluctance to be different from his friends, and, on the other, a rejection of being part of what he knew to be a trained killing organisation.

On his way to the shed one morning, he was handed a white

feather by an elderly lady who stated, "I think this is appropriate for you, young man." This incident left him so embarrassed that he reported to the recruiting office the next day, where he was examined by a doctor, who reported that he was physically unfit for the army as he had flat feet. This had never bothered him in his work in the cab, but he was nevertheless relieved, and was given a lapel badge 'For King and Country', to indicate that he was unavailable for military service.

He was sent in late 1914 to Northallerton, where he fired on freight trains and later on passenger trains, ferrying soldiers to and from the nearby Catterick Camp. With the increasing shortage of men for railway service, his promotion to Driver came quickly, initially staying on the same route and driving a variety of locomotives, from the small J21 0-6-0 tank engines to Worsdell's big 4-4-2 express locomotives for the heavier troop trains. Although still relatively young as a driver, he was competent, and his familiarity with a range of different locomotives made him a welcome addition to any shed.

One morning on a troop train to Catterick Camp, he had a young passed cleaner, William Thorpe, firing for him. He had met William before, but had not worked with him. The train was only moderately heavy, and they had a J21 0-6-0 locomotive, and Michael wondered how the young lad would manage. Although Passed Cleaner, William Thorpe would not have been his choice as fireman. He was a good lad but rather inexperienced and prone to agitation when things got beyond him, like just now, thought Michael.

"What the 'ell do I do now?" gasped William. A large lump of coal had jammed in the fire hole of their engine, and he couldn't shift it with his shovel.

"Get the coal hammer, you daft ha'porth," laughed Michael. "You should've known better than to try and shove that big lump into the firebox. Give it a few belts with the hammer, and be quick about it; we'll soon be losing steam pressure, else."

Grabbing the coal hammer, William gave the lump of coal a swift thump to try and break it, but the coal resisted and refused to ease its grip on the fire hole. Lifting the hammer once more, he smacked it down on the piece of coal again and this time a corner broke off.

"You're getting' there, William," chuckled the driver, "A few more belts, and you'll have it in the firebox!" And with this encouraging remark, Driver Timson turned back to his own side of the cab, and glanced out of the cab side to check on the signal they were approaching.

"You're in luck, William!" he called out. "We've got the distant against us, and we might have the home against us, too. That'll give you time to sort your coal problem." The home signal was also against them, so William was able to settle the fire to Michael's satisfaction, and then get on to the tender and break up a few more big lumps before they too could get stuck in the firebox door. Michael looked on with approval before the home signal dropped again for them to proceed into the next section; it seemed that his young mate was learning quickly.

When they stopped at Catterick, to let the troops out and reload with more for the return journey, William was quick to hop down to the track to change the headlamps and uncouple the engine from its train so that it was ready to move off before backing down alongside their coaches to couple on again at the other end; they were to travel tender-first on the return journey. This was completed without further incident, and Michael had noticed how William had managed his duties with care, if not always as quickly as an experienced man would have done. In spite of this, thought Michael to himself, he would be quite happy to have the lad again as a fireman.

The two enginemen were sometimes booked to take trains from the coast at Hull or Tyneside across to Fusehill Military Hospital in Carlisle. Driver Timson was often requested by the medical staff on the long run with wounded sailors or infantrymen, because they appreciated his efforts to run trains carefully and without any unnecessary jerking. This once got him into trouble with railway management: on one occasion, when he had a heavy train full of badly wounded sailors returning from the Battle of Jutland, and ran his train so carefully that he arrived in Carlisle over twenty minutes late.

This caused minor disruption to the timetable and both men

were called to account by an angry platform inspector.

"Was your late arrival due to incompetence on the part of your young fireman, Driver Timson?"

"Not at all, sir. He may be young but he is perfectly capable of doing what is required."

"I see. Then do you realise, Timson, that your late arrival in Carlisle Citadel Station has made several other train departures very late? This even includes the Scotch Express. The Glasgow & South Western engine had been kept waiting and the train arrived in Glasgow half an hour late. It had at least thirty important businessmen on board! This will be noted on your record."

"I'm really sorry, sir. Do you feel that inconvenience to a few businessmen is more important than the lives of two hundred sailors... sir?"

"Get out of my office!"

"Sir."

On their way back to the shed, William Thorpe was worried. "Will you be demoted back to the shovel, Mr Timson?"

"I doubt it, William, there are too few drivers already. Furthermore, if I am hauled up before the divisional superintendent, I will ask for witnesses from the army medical staff. If the Super doesn't like it, I'll resign and join the army's Non-Combatant Corps, and see how he likes that!" The NCC was a new unit in the British Army, which employed conscientious objectors in non-fighting roles.

Over the next few weeks, there was no indication that the inspector had taken any action. Carlisle's NER shedmaster said nothing, and Michael's duties did not change. He and Fireman Thorpe continued to work every few weeks, with an ambulance train hauled by one of Worsdell's very capable D20 4-4-0 locomotives. They were also taking troop trains between Carlisle, Durham and Berwick, to be handed over to the North British Railway there.

Early one evening, they were bringing an ECS (empty carriage stock) train from North Shields to Newcastle, and had left the terminus only twenty minutes earlier, when they heard a strange rumbling sound above the regular beat of their engine. Michael peered out of the cab to see a large cigar-shaped aerial vehicle following them, several hundred feet higher than them, and half a mile behind them.

"Good God, William, we've got a bloody Zeppelin chasing us!" he gasped. They had not been speeding, and the Zeppelin was slowing catching up with them, presumably to unload a bomb or two on their train. He stared ahead at the signals and saw that although the near home signal was clear, allowing them to enter the next section, the distant signal beyond it showed danger.

"Get shovelling, William; we're going to need more steam," said Michael, "and I want you to watch the line ahead carefully. We're going to ignore that distant, and try and get into the tunnel not far off beyond it; we might be able to hide from the bugger."

William checked the firebox, throwing another two shovelfuls of coal in to maintain whatever steam Michael needed (and being careful not to blacken the fire), and then leaned out of the cab to watch for anything on the track ahead, that could force them to stop. By the time they reached the tunnel, the Zeppelin was only a hundred yards behind them, but still too late to be able to drop a bomb. Once in the tunnel, Michael braked the train hard, but their speed had been too great for the train to stop completely in the tunnel. The locomotive and the leading coach protruded, and the two men scanned the sky anxiously.

"Nip out, William, and climb up above the tunnel mouth, and see if you can see where he is," Instructed his driver. William did so, then waved and shouted down that the aircraft was still in sight, but was flying back to the coast.

"Thank God for that!" muttered Michael. He was shaken by the narrow squeak they had had. Even if they had been bombed, only the two enginemen and the guard at the rear of the train would have been in danger; the train was otherwise empty. Their only problem now was to explain to a disbelieving signalman why they had passed his warning signal at speed. This turned out to be easy, however, because he had seen the Zeppelin following them, and had reported it.

"That was quick thinking, Driver Timson," commented the

shedmaster when they reported off duty that night. "I have noted it in your record."

"Thank you, sir; it might help to weaken the report about my recent late arrival with an ambulance train."

"Oh, don't worry about that. I replaced that with a commendation on your driving we received from the Royal Army Medical Corps. Inspector Ross is a pompous ass. A Midland Railway official at Leeds is proving to be difficult, and Ross has been transferred to Leeds to liaise with him. That should keep him out of our hair for a while."

"Very glad to hear it, sir."

9 - "Pride comes before a fall" (Nov 1917)

Young Archibald Hetherington was impetuous at all he did; nobody could have any doubts about that. Whatever he set his mind to was done with speed and excessive enthusiasm. This was a pity, as it sometimes meant that necessary advice on the matter in hand was not adhered to, or even heard. Consequently, the results did not always repay the intention. A case in point occurred on his tenth birthday on 11th May 1892. His parents had bought him a little model steam engine.

"Now then, Archie, Daddy will show you how to fire it," said his father, holding the lighter taper near little nozzle leading to the methylated spirits trough under the boiler, but little Archie was having none of it. He could see for himself how it worked, and reached eagerly for the taper.

"No Daddy, let me!" Archie's face showed his impatience. Mr Hetherington paused; he was wondering whether to let the lad fire the engine himself and burn his fingers, or insist on the boy curbing his patience, and seeing how it should be done. In the event, he didn't have to decide: his wife came in.

"Don't let him hurt himself, Robert. You know we'll have to take him to the doctor if he does, and he'll make such a fuss again, like last time."

But neither parent realised quite how quite determined their young son was. Before they could react, he had grabbed the burning taper, and thrust it directly into the trough, instead of into the nozzle. The methylated spirits caught fire with a *whump!* making Archie jump back in fright, banging his head on the chair behind, and immediately wailing at the resulting pain. The engine, now a mass of flames, tipped over, spilling its flaming mixture of methylated spirits and water over the carpet.

"Archie, you naughty boy, look at the mess you made!" wailed his mother. "Robert, we'll have to have the whole carpet replaced!"

His father took off his jacket and beat out the flames, grimly wondering whether he should also take off his belt to his son.

But over the following years, neither chastisement nor patience seemed to have any effect on curbing the boy's fervent wilfulness. In 1896, at the age of fourteen, he joined the London, Brighton & South Coast Railway as a cleaner, assuming that within five years the L B & S C R would recognise his ability, and he would become a driver speeding the luxury Southern Belle train between London and Brighton.

Yet it wasn't long before the senior cleaner at the Three Bridges engine shed complained to the shedmaster about the young man's impatience.

"Aye, well the lad's still young, Joseph. Let him learn the hard way. Give him a job where he might regret his impatience, without doing himself or the railway any serious damage."

"What sort of job had you in mind, sir?"

"Show him how to open the door on a coal wagon. Undo one bolt, and don't try to stop him from grabbing the second one."

A slow smile spread over the senior cleaner's face. "Aye; that might work."

A day or so later, another cleaner came looking for Archie. "Hey-up, young Hethers. The senior cleaner wants you for a job. He's with the coal wagons."

Archie hastily dropped the bucket of sand he was carrying, leaving it for someone else to trip over, and scurried over to the coal siding, where five newly arrived loaded coal wagons were waiting to be emptied.

"I need you to help me with these coal wagons, Hetherington. They have to be emptied, and the coal shovelled onto the staithes. First, you've got to undo both bolts like this," said the cleaner, undoing the left hand bolt, "and then—"

"Yessir, I've got it!" called Archie, grabbing the second bolt and sliding it out of its clip. Immediately, the door fell open, missing Archie's arm by an inch and pouring coal all over his legs and feet, until he was standing knee-deep in a heap of coal. Other cleaners had been warned, and were standing around waiting to see what happened. They all laughed as they saw the coal pour out. But again, Archie's misdemeanour had little effect on his lack of self-control, and further minor incidents continued to occur.

One Tuesday, after four years' service at Three Bridges, Archie was called over by the foreman cleaner. "Hetherington, I need you for a special duty further south. Horsham is short of a good cleaner, and I have suggested you for the job. You can start there on Monday next. It's not far, of course, so you can keep your present digs."

"Yessir!" Archie liked the sound of this: he had been described publicly as a 'good cleaner', and this boded well for his future. He was not aware that he was being disposed of as an embarrassment to the shed.

Horsham was a different shed, but the duties of a cleaner were much the same. Yet again progress for him was agonisingly slow. He maintained his enthusiastic approach, assuming that sooner or later someone in authority would see what the senior men in Three Bridges apparently could not: that he had the potential to be a fine engineman. It was 1913 before he was made up to Fireman, but even then he was kept in the lowest link, often involved in local shunting duties, or local runs on elderly tank engines. Such work was not onerous, and did not tax his ability unduly.

"Can't we go any faster, Mr Jermyn?" he asked petulantly on a slow goods as far as East Grinstead one afternoon.

"No Archie, we can't," replied Driver Jermyn, who was getting tired of this young fireman. "And don't pile so much coal into the firebox; you'll blacken the fire, and we've already got enough steam for what we need. You know very well that our pay is docked if we use more coal than is allowed for this run."

"Yes, but—"

"No buts! Think, boy, think! We have a timetable to keep to, and if we're early, awkward questions are going to be asked. Then the fire-dropper at Tunbridge Wells West is not going to be happy if he has a box full of fire to deal with."

Archie changed the subject: "When will we be working on tender engines? We always seem to be on tank engines."

"We work on what we're given," Driver Jermyn replied curtly.

Due to its south central position servicing London and the South Coast, the mainstay of the L B & S C R was passenger traffic, supplying the southern suburbs of London with a busy commuter service from both London Bridge and Victoria, as well as a country service reaching from Tunbridge Wells and St Leonards in the east to Guildford and Portsmouth in the west. A large proportion of these trains were hauled by tank engines, rather more so than with most of the other big main line companies. Even the pride of the line, the luxury Southern Belle Pullman train, was often hauled by the heavy J1 class 4-6-2T locomotive.

However, in early 1914, things began to look up, Archie thought. Men were joining the army as war in Europe seemed imminent. Archie himself was not interested in a 'patriotic duty', and ignored the pointing finger of Lord Kitchener on placards everywhere. He had no interest in shooting, or being shot at. Furthermore, having now been made up to fireman, he felt that he had a better chance of promotion now that so many men were leaving.

The war had put heavy demands on the railways in the UK, and none more so than on the London, Brighton & South Coast railway. In common with the South East & Chatham and the London & South Western Railways, there had been War Office requirements for hundreds of troop and ammunition trains to Southampton, Portsmouth, Newhaven, Folkstone and Dover, and then to bring back the wounded in ambulance trains. This extra pressure on the timetable caused severe disruptions to the London commuter services.

But these were not the only problems which worried the L B & S C R. Recruiting for the war effort had removed a large number of employees from railway service. Experienced railwaymen could be blocked from volunteering due to their status as 'reserved occupation' by the management of the various companies because they were needed to maintain essential services. Applications to serve in the armed forces from such men could only be accepted if they were accompanied by written permission from their seniors, and such permission was rarely given. This limitation, however, did not apply to engine cleaners, junior office staff, ostlers and farriers (the latter were in high demand in the army), or permanent way labourers. As a result, all railway companies were deprived of many valuable workers. But this did not affect Archie, now that he was a fireman.

He was quite certain that he could handle the promotion to firing from cleaning. He had fired before, of course, on several occasions, and had not disgraced himself, which probably explained why he had been considered for advancement, but all of his firing experience had been on tank engines, including once as an emergency fireman on one of the big 4-6-2T tank engines. Firing on a tender engine was another matter: you had to move across the fall plate to the tender to collect a shovelful of coal, then bring it back to the firebox. This required a different approach to firing. Furthermore, when the coal level at the tender front became low, you had to climb onto the heap at the back of the tender, and shovel enough coal forward so that it could be more easily accessed from the cab.

Although his driver, Alf Jones, also only recently promoted, was ready with good advice when he felt it appropriate, Archie still had very limited experience. But the exigencies of war had ensured that promotions were fast in these dark days.

In his first fortnight as a formal fireman, Archie was paired with Alf in both freight and passenger services from Horsham. At the end of the second week, their last duty of the day was to relieve a Littlehampton crew on a C2x 0-6-0 with the stopping passenger to London Bridge, and returning in the evening with the same locomotive as far as Horsham, where another Littlehampton crew would take over. Most C2 0-6-0 goods engines were unsuitable for passenger work, as they had no steam brakes, but these had been added to some, which were then re-classified C2x and could be used on passenger trains.

"First time I've fired on a tender engine, Mr Jones," remarked Archie cheerfully to his driver.

"Really?" Alf Jones was concentrating on his driving. "Then you'll know to take extra care if you're standing on the coal and we're approaching a bridge..."

"Yeah, I know!" interrupted Archie quickly, fearing he was about to get a lecture. He was a formal fireman now, he thought, and didn't need to be told how to do his job. He bent to examine the fire, to see where the next shovelful of coal was to go, and to avoid having to listen to advice. He didn't need advice on how to fire. He was enjoying his work and the acceleration of the train through the darkening countryside was exhilarating.

On leaving Epsom, Archie noticed that the coal was running low, and he climbed quickly up the coal at the back of the tender to shovel some forward for the last few miles. It was now dark, and his driver was watching for the signals. Archie shovelled enough coal forward, and then stood up on the remaining coal to climb down, just as they ran under a road bridge. The keystone of the bridge took his head off instantly, and it was thrown onto the track. Driver Jones did not immediately notice that Archie was missing, in fact not until near Dorking.

"Archie, the fire's low," he called, "get some more co-?" He caught sight of the headless body of his fireman on the tender. "Great God almighty!"

At Dorking, the station staff were informed of the missing head, and a search was undertaken. They found it next to the track by the bridge.

Archibald Hetherington had enjoyed his Fireman status for two weeks.

10 - "Not my problem now!" (May 1919)

In the spring of 1919, there was a distinct air of unease among employees of the many railway companies in the United Kingdom. The government had taken control of them from 1914, to ensure co-operation in the interests of efficient working during the Great War. In any case, by 1918 many of the companies had suffered financially, after the years of unremitting hard work and poor maintenance, and also due to increasing local bus competition. Indeed, the largest company, the London & North Western Railway was soon to be bought by its rival, the Lancashire & Yorkshire (although the former was to retain its name). The Railways Act of 1921 enacted a merger of almost all companies into four huge ones, each responsible for a specific area of the country. This was to take place on 1st January 1923. As a result, a good deal of employee redundancy was to be expected as the Big Four, as they became to be known, began to co-ordinate and re-arranged their hitherto independent companies. These were not the only problems.

The peace expected after the 'War to end all wars' had of course arrived, but the rewards, anticipated especially by many of those in the trenches who had, after all, done most of the fighting, had not. Resentment and even anger at poor employment conditions were not helped when many women, who had taken over railwaymen's duties during the hostilities, wished to retain their jobs. Now that the big railway mergers were due, even more unemployment was to be expected in railway circles. This was of particular concern to those smaller companies whose management had been comfortably inefficient without local rivals in public transport. These problems were already making themselves felt in the early summer of 1919 in the Cambrian Railway Company in North Wales.

Driver Emrys Pugh of Oswestry was not looking forward to his next shift; he was over sixty, and looking forward to his retirement. He was taking a Whitchurch to Pwllheli express as far as Barmouth; although what the Cambrian meant by the word 'express' was that it didn't stop at all stations. Much of the Cambrian was hilly, and the concept of speed as understood by the North-Western or the Great Western was a foreign concept.

Emrys was waiting at Oswestry's Cambrian Station for the two-coach connecting train from Gobowen to arrive at the neighbouring GWR terminus. The GWR's main Paddington to Birkenhead route passed within two miles of Oswestry, but their expresses only stopped at Gobowen, to allow passengers to change and take the six-minute run to Oswestry, where they could connect with Cambrian trains to the coastal towns and resorts at Aberystwyth, Barmouth, Pwllheli, or even South Wales.

"Here it comes, Mr Pugh," called Fireman Ianto Evans, as he saw the smoke from the approaching tank engine rounding the curve into the GWR terminus.

"At least the GWR is on time," muttered Emrys Pugh to himself. The Cambrian was not a system noted for its punctuality; its own hilly routes with dubious weather tended to limit this. Their own train for the coast had connected with the mighty LNWR at Whitchurch. He and his fireman, Ianto Morris, had boarded their train there and had passengers from Liverpool and Manchester eager to sample the Welsh coastal resorts after the wartime restrictions on holiday travel.

GWR Passengers were now hurrying to board the train, but one young fellow came up to the engine, saw Ianto, and called out, "This 'ere the Creeckut train, Wack?" Ianto frowned; he didn't understand the Liverpudlian accent. Most of the staff on the Cambrian spoke Welsh, and Ianto's English left something to be desired; and what was this about cricket? He shook his head and turned to his driver.

Emrys leaned over and called to the passenger, "Yes, but you will have to change trains at Barmouth for Criccieth."

"Ta!" And the young man went to find himself a seat in the train.

"What does he mean by 'ta', Mr Pugh? And why did he call me Wack?" asked his young fireman in Welsh, their normal mode of conversation.

"Ta's a short way of saying 'thank you' that the Saesneg use," smiled Emrys, "and 'Wack' is Liverpool for friend." Even after fifteen hundred years, the Welsh still referred to the English as Saxons, as indeed did the Scots, who referred to them as Sassenachs.

"I don't think I will ever really understand their language," grumbled Ianto.

"Give yourself time, Ianto, it'll come one day."

Soon, they had the guard's flag, as the joining passengers had boarded the train, and Driver Hughes lifted the regulator of his Aston designed '16' class 4-4-0 passenger locomotive for their run to Barmouth. Here, they would come off duty and hand the train over to a Pwllheli crew. Although not a long run by the standards of the larger railway companies such as the Midland or the Lancashire & Yorkshire, it was tiring. Driver Hughes had done it many times, and knew it well. However, he was beginning to look forward to the time when he could stop work, perhaps when more men came home from the war.

The short run from Whitchurch had warmed up the engine well, but the next stretch consisted of a number of stops and starts, so that the crew could not get up a clear run to Welshpool. Both men were kept busy either starting or preparing to stop, first at Llynclys, junction for the Llangynog branch, followed very soon by another stop at Llanymnech for the Llanfyllin branch, before arriving at Welshpool Junction, where passengers for Llanfair Caereinion could disembark. Emrys smiled to himself at the thought of any English crewmen from the GWR who might be sent to ex-Cambrian routes, and who would have to handle the names of these towns and villages; names which were simplicity itself for the native Welsh.

Shortly after leaving Welshpool, Emrys remarked to his fireman, "I especially like this next section, Ianto, I find this hilly area full of interest."

They were held up at a signal for several minutes. While they waited, Ianto checked the fire and the steam pressure, then gazed up into the hills, where he could see a flock of sheep in the distance, with the shepherd and his dog chivvying them higher up. Closer to them, there was a patch of longer grass, with what looked like a pale boulder in it. "Odd-looking boulder there, Mr Pugh," he remarked, "Looks like a porker's got into the field."

Emrys moved over to look. "That's not a pig," he said, considering. At that moment, they heard the frantic bark of the sheepdog as it came racing down towards the 'boulder', which stood up to reveal itself to be a young man devoid of clothing below the waist. He grabbed his trousers, helped up a young lady rapidly adjusting a petticoat, and the pair of them hurried away, with the dog in pursuit. Only four or five yards ahead of the dog the pair reached a stone wall, scrambled over it and disappeared, with the angry, distant shepherd waving his crook at them. Emrys moved back to the regulator, grumbling about the laxity of morals brought about by the recent war, while Ianto held firmly onto the handrail on the left of the cab, helpless with laughter. "I have to agree with you, Mr P," he gasped, "this hilly section is definitely full of interest!"

The next section had fewer stops, but at one Emrys looked around carefully. This was Cemmes Road, junction for the short branch to Dinas Mawddwy. He and Glenys had talked about retiring there one day, and for Emrys that day couldn't come soon enough. He was very tired of the excessive demands of wartime driving, with its heavy troop trains and long runs with ill-maintained locomotives. The Cambrian had never been a prosperous line, and had not been able to afford to build its own locomotives, and those which it had were getting well past their best.

After the run, Emrys decided that he would not wait any longer, and applied for a transfer to a quieter duty; he had heard that a driver at Cemmes Road was due to retire, and he put a word in the ear of a member staff he knew office at the head office in Oswestry. His application was approved, and he and Glenys sold their house in Oswestry and moved to Dinas Mawddwy. Emrys joined the roster there, and spent the next two years mainly on the quiet run on the local branch, with only occasional duties to Aberystwyth or Barmouth.

It was in late the afternoon on 31st December 1922, when Emrys had his final run as Driver. The following day, the Cambrian would not exist, having merged with the Great Western Railway, like most other smaller Welsh railways. Emrys had decided that this was a good time to retire. For some drivers, their very last run was accompanied by a certain degree of nostalgia for a profession they had pursued for many years, but not for Driver Hughes. He was looking forward to the chance of settling down with Glenys in their little house in Mawddwy. He would no longer be required to get up at ungodly hours to work trains through the Welsh valleys in the winter snows, with all the concomitant problems that were to be expected on such runs. He would no longer be condemned to spend hours shunting on freezing cabs with little or no protection from the rain or snow. After today, whenever he heard the whistle of the early morning departure of the local passenger to Cemmes Road, he could sit back in his armchair, enjoying his tea, and thank the Lord that he was no longer the poor diafol having to drive it, and this added a certain flavour to his tea and rarebit!

In fact, his only minor regret was that of losing contact with his young fireman, whose company he had learned to value. Ianto was, Emrys knew, a man with a railway future. With the merger with the GWR, Ianto was to be retained; he was already a fine and competent fireman, who would one day become a first-rate driver, if Emrys was any judge of the matter.

These and similar thoughts were running through Emrys' mind as he drew his train slowly to a halt at Cemmes Road. Ianto dropped from the cab to uncouple the coaches, and Emrys eased the locomotive forward to the points, to prepare to set back along the release line to the other end of the train in order for Driver Mervyn Thomas, his relieving driver, to take it back to Mawddwy, this time with Emrys as a passenger. Mervyn climbed aboard from the platform and shook Emrys' hand. They did not say much to each other; Emrys regarded Mervyn as a lazy and rather shiftless man who did not take his duties very seriously. Mervyn eased the regulator up very slightly to take the engine back past the coaches, then braked very suddenly, stopping the engine as he remembered the single line token for the run back to Mawddwy. He climbed down off the engine to collect it from the signalman waiting on the platform. But the engine brake had not been correctly applied, and the engine rolled slowly past its train, along the main line (for which the points had been set), along down the gentle downhill grade towards Machynlleth. Mervyn knew he had enough time to hurry along the platform with the token and climb back on the engine before it reached the points to reverse again back onto its train.

Emrys, at a window seat, saw the engine go past and noticed that the cab was empty. He half stood up, but then saw Mervyn hurrying past with the token and realising what the man was doing, shook his head, muttering a short (and unmentionable) Welsh expression. He got out of the train to see whether Mervyn could catch the engine. Ianto, meanwhile, had walked to the other end of the train and was waiting by the first coach, to couple up again when the engine was backed onto its train.

Mervyn, however, had been stopped by an attractive young lady with a question; he paused, smiled, and began to answer, before he recalled why he had been hurrying. He began to run, staring his engine as it passed the reversing points, and continuing on its leisurely way down the main line, now well out of his reach. This light engine without anyone in its cab was to run several miles down the line and reach Machynlleth before anyone was able to board and apply its brakes.

Emrys was now out on the platform, shaking his head sadly. Mervyn came back to him. "Emrys, what the hell do I do now?" he asked in desperation. Emrys shook his head, "Don't ask me, boyo, I'm no longer a railway employee. It's not my problem." He turned and climbed back into the train, and, opening his paper again, sat down and began to read it.

11 - A matter of honour
(June 1933)

Southern Railway Driver Alan Watson, of Stewarts Lane shed in south London, was a quiet, sedate man in his late fifties. He was sitting in the cab of a Lord Nelson class locomotive, waiting at the head of the Southern's crack Golden Arrow train at Dover Marine. The weather in the Channel was decidedly boisterous, with rain squalls, choppy waves, and gusting winds. The captain of the ferry from Calais had done a marvellous job of getting his ship into the harbour, bringing his passengers in to disgorge them only three minutes later than scheduled. The crossing had been rough, and he'd had to wait a further five minutes before he could bring his ship safely to the quayside.

The Golden Arrow with its ten first-class-only Pullman coaches hauled by the big 4-6-0 locomotive was waiting ready to take its passengers on their ninety-eight-minute journey to the London terminus at Victoria.

Driver Watson, gazing down the platform at the arriving passengers, turned to his mate, Fireman Joe Hinchcliffe. "We should easily be able to make up the delay, Joe. That captain's done a good job in this weather."

His fireman was new to this run, and although he had known Alan Watson for some time, he had not fired to him before, but he already 'knew the road' between Dover and Victoria. Enginemen were not normally permitted to work over any route which they had not officially learned.

"Yes, he has," replied Joe, "look at them waves still!"

Both men could see the whitecaps across all of the waves out at sea, and there were pale faces among the crowd of passengers hurrying onto the platform. Among them they noted a very well-known film actor, and a couple of society beauties, frequently seen in the pages of magazines read only by the sort of passenger who could afford to travel on their train. Joe gave a final check to the steam pressure and the fire, while Alan took his watch from his waistcoat pocket to check the time. Driver Watson had a private ambition to bring the Golden Arrow exactly on time for his tenth consecutive run to Victoria. His previous nine runs had been successful in this regard, and he had his fingers crossed that there would be no reason to prevent this from happening on his tenth.

Finally, the guard sounded his whistle and Alan reached for the regulator, eased it gently upwards, and the train moved smoothly away out of the platform, only eight minutes behind time.

"Nice," commented Joe. Not all drivers could handle the Lord Nelsons, which had a tendency to be difficult to drive, and in wet weather with a heavy train they could experience a thunderous wheel-slip as the driving wheels failed to grip on the wet rails. But in experienced hands – and Driver Watson was very experienced - they could be exceptionally good engines. They had originally been built for the heavy expresses on the Southern, and the 460-ton boat trains from Dover to Victoria needed the most powerful locomotives the Southern had. At their appearance in 1926, the Southern was able to boast that it now had the most powerful express passenger locomotives in Britain, surpassing the Great Western's Castle class engines. The Great Western immediately responded by producing their King class, instantly putting the Lord Nelsons in the shade. Unfortunately, the Southern had only sixteen of these engines; not enough for many enginemen to train on them. Furthermore, their long fireboxes made 'learning on the job' very tricky. Still, on this particular day, Alan had his locomotive well in hand, and the train was able to get away quickly, so that its two enginemen were hopeful of being able to make up the lost time.

The first section of the journey to London was along the coastal cliffs towards Folkestone, but here the weather provided more problems as the stormy sea sent spray over the tracks adding to the rain.

"Hmm," muttered Alan, wiping his eyes, "I can't see the signals well. You have a look, Joe, and see if they're clear for us. They should be, because we're the most important train along here today."

Joe looked out, but, although their locomotive had recently been fitted with new smoke deflectors, these had no effect on the spray across the tracks. "Sorry, Mr Watson, I can't see 'em as clearly as I'd like, either."

Alan slowed his train slightly; one couldn't take any risks with this particular train. By the time they passed Folkestone, they had lost three more minutes. But soon the route turned northwest, away from the coast and into the hills, and the wind and rain eased off. Alan increased the speed to try to make up the lost minutes. Checking with the station clock against their standard issue watches as they raced through Ashford, they noticed that they had already regained four of the minutes, and the train was running well, encouraging both enginemen to anticipate regaining the final minutes.

A few miles beyond Ashford, Alan, with his hand on the regulator, smiled at his mate. "We might just do this, Joe, she's running in fine style!" he said. "Let's hope so, Mr W," replied his fireman as he put four more shovelfuls of coal in the centre of the long firebox exactly where the coal would work its way down to the front. "She's behaving herself well!"

But they spoke too soon; Alan checked out of the cab once again to see the next home signal was clear, but the distant signal on the gantry bracket was at danger.

"Oh dear!" he said as his annoyance level rose. "What is the signal bobby doing? He should be giving us priority over everything!" However, in this case the signalman was not at fault: the engine of a slow freight had been failed by its crew, and a replacement engine was easing the freight into a refuge siding, to clear the way for the express. By the time the freight had been installed safely into the refuge and the signal cleared for their train, they had lost more time and were now running twelve minutes behind time, with a frustrated driver at the helm.

Joe Hinchliffe was aware of his driver's wish to achieve his tenth run on time, and was quietly wondering to himself whether he was going to hear Alan express himself in dubious language. Alan was well known throughout Stewarts Lane shed for being a man with the patience of Job, and a man who eschewed bad language. Yet, thought Joe, this run was stretching even Alan's patience.

After recovering from the signal check, favourable signals allowed the driver to build up speed once more, and they were soon racing through the Kent countryside. There was an increasingly satisfied expression on Alan Watson's face as he took out his watch from time to time. He nodded to his mate, saying, "We're getting those minutes back, Joe. We'll only be five minutes down through Tonbridge, and we should be able to regain them too before Victoria!"

But here, Driver Watson was in error: a coach on a local train at Tonbridge Station had derailed on the main up line, and a Permanent Way gang was busy re-railing the coach, resulting in a re-routing of the express through the station's main down line. This required a 'Wrong Line' order to be issued, and a consequent slowing of their progress through the station itself. Joe Hinchcliffe took a guarded glance at his driver, but only saw the man's lips grimly pressed together. Joe shook his head in quiet appreciation of his driver's determined self-control.

But after the delay, Joe noticed a change in Alan Watson's demeanour. "I'm going to need your best firing, Joe," he said curtly. "We're going to run." And run they did. Driver Watson was like a robot, instantly reacting to every variation on the track, and keeping an impressive control of the regulator. Joe had never seen such skill. He had long known that Alan Watson was a good driver, but this demonstration was train control at its very best. The word must have gone through the signalmen along the line as well, because now every signal was set at clear for them. By the time they were nearing the bridge over the Thames, half a mile from Victoria, Alan had regained every lost minute, and as they began to descend the short gradient down to the terminus, they were on time. Then, a mere four hundred yards short of the station, the emergency brakes went on and the train came to a squealing stop, to the shock of both enginemen.

"Some bastard's pulled the communication chord!" gasped Joe. "Why the hell pull it here?"

It was several minutes before the guard reported to them that a passenger in a toilet had fallen ill, and, unaware of how close they were to the station, had pulled the chord, thus stopping the train. Without any comment, Driver Watson restarted the train and took it gently into the terminus. His tenth run had arrived at Victoria fifteen minutes late.

Back at the Stewarts Lane shed, many drivers had wished Alan luck in his attempt to run the train on time for ten consecutive days, and now commiserated with him. They all knew from long personal experience that such things happened to enginemen, and that there was nothing to be done about it. You just had to grin and bear it.

A week later, a letter appeared in one of the national dailies. It was written by the actor, who had missed an important engagement due to the lateness of the train. He wrote that he had another meeting in Paris in two months' time, and expected to return once more on the Golden Arrow; but on his next arrival in Dover, he proposed to enquire the name of the train's driver and, if it was the same man, then he would refuse to board the train and travel instead by bus.

Joe showed the paper to Alan, who read it then said quietly, "He hasn't heard the last of this!"

Another letter was published in the same newspaper a few days later, this time from Driver Watson. It expressed his regret that the actor had missed his business meeting, but explained that the circumstances causing the train's delay were external to the train, and in any case had no relationship whatever to his, the driver's, competence. He added that should a film starring the aforementioned actor be screened at his local cinema, neither he nor his wife would be going to see it.

Later that same week in Stewarts Lane shed, Alan arrived on duty with a gentle smile on his face.

"You look like a cat that's got the cream, Mr W," said Joe. "Why's that?"

Alan gave him a letter. "This arrived this morning," he said. "Have a read."

Joe opened the letter and took out a sheet of paper. It was a handwritten note from the actor personally. It expressed his sincere apology for the misunderstanding, and assured Driver Watson that in future the actor would be very happy to sit in any train that Alan would be driving. But there was more: two tickets for luxury seats in the cinema at Leicester Square (where one of the actor's films was screening) were included. There were also two paid bookings for a night and dinner at London's exclusive

Dorchester Hotel, and a cheque for five pounds to cover any travel or other expenses the driver and his wife might incur.

"Honour," said Alan Watson, "is satisfied!"

12 - Beginning can be difficult
(August 1935)

George Dunkworth MA, history teacher, was boring the boys in his third form to tears. He was even able to bore them with the explanation of why Henry VIII had Queen Anne beheaded; a topic which any half-decent historian could make fascinating. Jerry Smith had his head down behind Fatty Thomas, where he was effectively invisible to the teacher, and was dozing quietly. Dai Gruffydd could not hide; the desk in front was empty, and most of what he did was easily visible from the teacher's rostrum.

Placing on his face what he hoped was an interested expression, Dai's hands beneath his desk held his wooden ruler and eased it across the aisle to poke his neighbour, Jerry Smith, who had recently moved to Chester from Yorkshire. Jerry jerked upright, the sudden movement catching Dunky's attention.

"Ha! Woken up, have we, Smith?" Dunky's grim smile promised trouble. "Two hundred lines by tomorrow morning: 'I must not sleep in history classes.'"

"Miserable sod!" muttered Dai, *sotto voce*.

Dunky's hearing was acute. "What was that, Gruffydd?"

"Er - nothing, sir."

"What did you say?"

"I was just commenting on your punishment, sir. I said 'Message from God.'"

Dunkworth could not decide whether this was a compliment or not and, prudently ignoring it, continued with his tedium.

Dai Gruffydd was not basically a bad boy, but his difficulty was that he was bored with school, and this was compounded by above-average intelligence. At thirteen, he had to wait another year before he could leave school and get a job, but in this year of 1935, jobs were not easy to come by.

On their way home, as he and Jerry were passing the local Saltney railway yard, they paused to watch a small engine shunt some wagons.

"I read a book called 'The Tower of London' by a bloke called Ainsworth. It were right excitin'" said Smith, "It were about Queen Jane wot reigned for on'y nine days."

"There was never a Queen called Jane. It's like havin' a queen called Pam or Doris," mocked Dai, "doesn't sound right for a queen."

"Straight it were; she an' 'er bloke were be'eaded by Queen Mary. Why the 'ell can't Dunky make 'istory worth lissenin' to?" Jerry complained.

Neither boy was aware that this wish was to be granted the following year.

As they watched the shunting, Dai pointed to the shunters working with their poles, coupling and uncoupling the wagons to the shouts and signals of the driver. One of the shunters ran alongside the moving train, shoved the pole between two wagons, and with a quick flick neatly uncoupled them, shouting to the driver, who immediately slowed the train and left the uncoupled wagons to carry on rolling along the track.

"That looks an easy job," Dai commented.

Jerry laughed at him. "'Ave you ever felt one o' them couplings?" he asked. "They're bloody 'eavy; I nipped in once last year, and tried to uncouple a wagon; it were too bleedin' 'eavy. That's flamin' 'ard work, that is."

"Still might be better than listening to old Dunky droning."

"Well I'm quite 'appy snoozin' behind Fatty's arse, when Dunky's teachin'."

Next year in the fourth form, they had Mr Hetherington teaching history; he made the subject far more interesting for the boys, and Dai began to pay more attention, but all this changed for him one morning. Mr Hetherington was away, and the replacement history teacher walked in. To Dai's bitter disappointment, it was Mr Dunkworth.

"Pleased to see me, I see, Gruffydd," remarked Dunky as he caught Dai's deflated expression.

"Can't honestly say that I am, sir," said Dai, "but I do have a question for you."

"How interesting. Let us hear it," smirked Dunky.

"Mr Hetherington only has a BA, sir, whereas you have an MA." Dunky nodded in appreciation. "So," continued Dai, "how is it that he makes history fascinating and you make it so bloody boring - sir?"

There was a shocked silence in the class. Dunky went white with anger. "Get out of this room, Gruffydd, and report instantly to the headmaster's office! I will see you there."

Dai slowly gathered his books and left the room.

The headmaster listened to the tirade from Dunky and asked Dai if the accusation was accurate. Dai admitted that it was.

"Thank you, Mr Dunkworth; I will deal with Gruffydd now. You may return to your class." The headmaster took out a sheet of paper and began to write. He finished the note and placed it into an envelope, which he sealed and handed it to Dai. "You will give this letter to your father, Gruffydd. It explains why from tomorrow you will no longer be attending this school."

Dai's parents were unimpressed at his expulsion. "Well, now you'll have to find work," said his father. "You can't expect us to pay for your upkeep if you don't do anything to help."

"Well, what can I do?" asked Dai.

"That, my son, is your problem. We will keep you for the next fortnight; after that, if you want to stay living here, you'll have to help."

Dai spent the whole day walking around looking for work, without any success; with the 1930s depression in full swing, unemployment was rife. He tried the Labour Exchange, and was given a number of possible jobs, but when he turned up they had all been taken. On his second day, he found casual work loading for a local coal haulier, and received two shillings for three days' work, which was appreciated by his parents, but the work was very heavy, very dirty, and didn't last.

A week later, he was once more pounding the streets on the off-chance of finding something, again without any luck. This continued for several months with varying degrees of success; even fifteen-year-olds had little chance against the large number of adults also looking for work. There was nothing very promising, until he remembered his conversation with Jerry Smith about work in a railway yard. His uncle was an engine driver with the

LMS and had come visiting once. He had told them about the excitement of driving a huge express locomotive at seventy miles an hour. Dai went to see the foreman at the nearby Chester GWR engine shed.

"Have you any Great Western connections, lad?" asked Mr Thompson.

"No, sir, but an uncle drives for the LMS."

"You interested in railways? Or are you just looking for work?"

"Both sir, if I'm honest."

"I'm sorry to disappoint you, but we really don't have any vacancies."

"Thank you for at least listening to me, sir. But I do have a question: this is a GWR shed, isn't it?"

"Yes, that's right."

"Well why is that LMS Black Five here? Chester's got an LMS shed as well. Shouldn't it be there?"

"Black Five?"

"Yeah, it's just beyond that single slip over on the right."

"Oh, that's just come in to be turned before we send it...?" He paused and then asked slowly, "Did you say single slip?"

"Yes, it's the one over-'

"I know where it is! What do you know about slips, single or double?"

"I think they're used to save space when planning tracks."

"Now, how did you know that? And how come you know what a Black Five is?"

"My dad has a model train layout, and he makes his own track."

The foreman sat back in his chair and gazed thoughtfully at Dai. "I know someone who could use a young lad like yourself, after all. He's the foreman cleaner in Ruabon. You'd probably get four bob a day. That suit you?"

Four shillings for a day's work was good money compared to what most of his working friends were getting, and Ruabon wasn't that far away.

"Yes, sir." Dai replied.

The foreman cleaner at Ruabon looked Dai up and down and asked. "Have you any railway experience, lad?"

"No, sir," replied Dai.

"Hmm, the shedmaster at Chester thinks you might have some potential." He thought for a moment, then said, "Look, I'll give you a week's trial and we'll see how you go. You will join Mr Ridley's gang."

"Thank you, sir."

There were four lads in Owen Ridley's cleaning gang. One cleaner with a grin on his face, called in Welsh, "Send him for a left-handed spanner, Owen!"

Dai asked, also in Welsh, "Would that be from the left-handed shed, Mr Ridley?"

There was a shout of laughter from the gang, and Owen Ridley smiled at him. "You'll do, Dai Gruffydd, you'll do!"

Over the next three years, Dai worked hard and became a formal cleaner in 1937. He also assisted occasionally on the footplate of engines, earning himself the odd packet of Woodbines from firemen by pulling coal forward in the tender while they sloped off for a quiet smoke. He was occasionally sent to Llangollen or Corwen too, when flu was doing the rounds. Much of the labouring work in this part of the Great Western system was conducted in Welsh; in some of the more remote villages, a few of the locals spoke no English.

One morning Dai was sent north along the main line to Chester shed, where a particularly heavy bout of flu had caused havoc. Here he found himself cleaning the big passenger 4-6-0s: Halls, Saints, and even Stars and Castles. The cleaning standards demanded on these engines were far stricter and he had his work cut out.

He was working on the tender of a Hall one morning as a Star passed slowly with its fireman looking out of the cab. He noticed Dai and called out, "Hey, you; shove that point lever over!" Dai could only see one point lever, which would switch the points ahead and guide the engine to the turntable. But the table wasn't set for the track.

"Which point lever?" Dai called.

"That one starin' at you, you daft git!" shouted the fireman angrily.

Dai shrugged, assuming the driver would stop before he reached the turntable, and switched the points over. The Star trundled along the track, reached the turntable edge, and its front bogie tipped into the well. There was instant consternation as the driver cursed his fireman, who indignantly pointed to Dai, who had changed the points.

Sidney Thompson appeared, calling for the nearby Hall driver to get his engine, to help drag the Star back out of its undignified position. He demanded to see all those involved, including Dai, in his office. "You have only been here a week, Gruffyd, and already you have derailed the engine for the 11.35 Paddington; thus delaying this express by at least an hour. Did you not see that the points switch would direct the engine into the turntable?"

"Yes, sir; but I assumed the driver would stop his engine."

"What would be the point of the engine moving a few yards further?"

"Er - I don't know, sir."

"I do not think the GWR can use a young man like yourself-?" He was interrupted by a knock on his door. "Come in." he called, annoyed. His annoyance did not abate when he saw who came in. "What do you want, Hargreaves? Can't you see I'm busy?"

"Yessir, but I saw wot 'appened, sir"

"Explain."

"The Star fireman tol' the lad 'ere ter change the points, but from where 'e wos, the lad cu'd on'y see one set o' points, an' they wasn't the points wot the fireman wanted changed... er- sir..."

"I see. That puts a very different light on the matter. Where is your driver, Hargreaves?"

"'E's outside on our engine, sir."

Mr Thompson went out to the engine. "Did you see what happened here, George?" he asked Driver Denton.

"No Sid, I didn't. But I know where the young cleaner was when it happened. He couldn't have seen the points the Salop fireman meant."

Later, Dai met the young fireman and held out his hand. "You saved my bacon today, mate. I'd like to thank you."

The fireman grinned and shook his hand. "Pleased ter

meetcher," he said, "Me name's Lance."

Dai stayed in Chester shed for several months during which time he was to hear a great deal about Lance Hargreaves and his driver, George Denton.

13 - A short stint as driver
(April 1942)

Fireman Bill Murgatroyd was becoming a bitter man: he had been a fireman for several years, and, in his opinion, longer than he ought to have been. He had, he believed, been due for promotion to at least Acting Driver years earlier. He had started his railway career at Manchester's LNER shed at Gorton as a cleaner, two years after the railway Grouping of 1923, and over the years he had managed to progress, albeit slowly, to Fireman.

The fact of the matter, however, was that Gorton shedmaster Barry Rickman had long had grave doubts about Fireman Murgatroyd's sense of responsibility, and was waiting until a more serious attitude in the man could show itself. So far, little had eventuated. Shedmaster Rickman had even hoped that Fireman Murgatroyd might apply for permission to join the army after the war had broken out in 1939. Barry could then agree to waive the requirement that an engineman was regarded as essential to railway service, and give his permission. But no such application had been received, and, in any case, Manchester was so short of enginemen that he could hardly afford to lose even any men, even of Murgatroyd's calibre. He had to put up with the man, as he had with others, Gorton shed being a large one, with many enginemen on the books. Shedmaster Rickman, in reality, needed every one of them; good, bad or indifferent.

However, as far as Fireman Murgatroyd was concerned, Rickman's problem appeared to solve itself in late January 1942. A notice had been posted in the enginemen's mess that several vacancies had occurred at York North, and enginemen were urged to apply if they wished to extend their route knowledge and experience. The shedmaster was pleased to see an application from Fireman Murgatroyd, and promptly counter-signed it in case the man changed his mind. Within a fortnight, Fireman Murgatroyd was gone.

York was not only a major change-over point on the King's Cross-Edinburgh route; it also had to supply enginemen for a number of shorter local routes to places like Harrogate, Leeds, Hull, and Yorkshire's East Coast towns such as Scarborough and Whitby. Fireman Murgatroyd was now able to add considerably to his route knowledge, which, he believed, should enhance his chance of further promotion. Furthermore, he assumed that York would be far less a target for the Luftwaffe than Manchester was. More than once, Bill, like so many others, had feared for his life as the bombs rained down on railway property. Several railwaymen had lost houses and even lives in 1940-41. Manchester, the Luftwaffe had made clear, continued to be a major target for its attention.

Bill Murgatroyd looked around his new shed with immense satisfaction. Gorton had been a big shed by any standard, but York North was huge. Here were several of the big Pacific class 4-6-2s, which were rare at Gorton: the main line between Manchester and Sheffield did not really warrant their use. York, on the other hand, was where engines on the Scottish expresses were sometimes changed. He hoped he would soon be allowed to fire one and, when his turn came, to even drive one. He realised of course that he would have to drive on the local lines first, before he could be permitted to drive the expresses, but he could wait, knowing that sooner or later he would get his chance. He was having to learn, he mused, as he placed another shovelful of coal into the firebox of the little tank engine of the 4.30pm to Harrogate, to be a patient man.

In his first few months at York, he travelled along most of the local routes to extend his knowledge and had fired to several drivers in the shunting and local links. But his extended route knowledge was not the only acquisition in his new position: he had also rapidly acquired a reputation among his drivers for his casual attitude to his firing duties. The York North shedmaster had been asked several times by drivers if there was an alternative fireman available when they found his name rostered with them. But the shedmaster's worries about the new fireman were put into the shade one evening in late April. The Luftwaffe came visiting.

Apart from damage inflicted on the city itself, the heavy raid on York had caused much destruction of the railway facilities. The engine shed at York North suffered with major damage to several engines, including one of its streamlined Pacifics; this locomotive had been so badly damaged as to make its repair or reconstruction unwarrantable, and it was set aside for scrapping. The raid had therefore seriously hampered the shed's ability to manage its role in providing locomotives for both the main and local routes. A significant proportion of the roster of enginemen had also been rendered unfit for duty. This required an urgent re-appraisal of the list of available enginemen, including Bill Murgatroyd. He had been fortunate, in that he had been off duty and in the Anderson shelter in the garden of his house during the raid.

He gazed in pleasure at the noticeboard in the enginemen's mess a fortnight after the raid. His name was there, on the promotion list to Acting Driver.

Finally! he thought to himself. *They've done the right thing - about bloody time, too!* He had long felt that he ought to have been a driver, but this view of his had apparently not been shared by management. Now due to the raid, his long wait had ended.

His first duty as an acting driver came the following day. He was to take a rake of empty goods wagons to Harrogate with an old J15 0-6-0 goods engine. These engines had originally been built by the Great Central Railway, and had proved to be useful and long-lived engines. His fireman was Ged Warcross; himself an old ex-driver who had retired in 1939 but had been accepted back into the LNER for the duration. Ged was an experienced engineman, and the shed master had thought to partner him with Acting Driver Murgatroyd to keep an eye on him for a few days.

The run from York to Harrogate was a short one, and the load none too demanding, but Bill was determined to show his competence and arrive in Harrogate either slightly ahead or, at least dead on, time. He fussed about the cab, changing the position of the regulator frequently to try and get the best out of the old engine.

"For God's sake, Bill, leave off your fuss! The old girl knows this road well enough, and doesn't need you to tell her what to do. Just relax and let her get on with it." Ged was normally a patient man, but his driver was getting on his nerves.

"Ged, you've forgotten something."

"What?"

"You're no longer a driver. I'm the driver, and I'll decide how to drive this train."

Ged Warcross just shrugged his shoulders and carried on with his firing, without another word. They ran through Knaresborough at a higher speed than was wise (or even permitted), and the empty wagons shook and clattered over the points, with the guard waving urgently from his van. The stationmaster at Knaresborough hurried out of his office to see what the noise was.

"The guard's waving at you to slow down," said Ged.

"Bugger the guard; he's not driving," muttered Bill.

They arrived in the yard at Harrogate ten minutes early, with Bill smiling as he noted the time in his notebook.

Two days later, he was called into the shedmaster's office.

"Acting Driver Murgatroyd, you were ten minutes ahead of time in Harrogate the other day. Can you explain this?"

"We had a good run, sir."

"Obviously. We also had a complaint from Knaresborough that your freight ran through at speed."

"I wasn't aware of any speed restriction, sir."

"Don't you read the day's instructions?"

"Yessir, of course."

"Then you missed that one. Didn't your fireman warn you? He's a very competent man."

"If he did, I missed it, sir."

"If you want to keep your promotion, Murgatroyd, you'll have to take far more care."

A week later, the shift notice indicated that he was again to take a train to Harrogate, this time the 7.20 am local passenger; an easy run with a D11 4-4-0 locomotive and six non-corridor coaches. His mate was Fireman Bertie Longbotham who had only served three years as fireman, but who was known to be a reliable, if taciturn, man.

Taking the locomotive from the shed to York station, Bill noted that the engine was not in the best of condition, but this was to be expected under the wartime circumstances, in which most sheds were short-staffed. Nevertheless, he felt proud to be sitting on the left-hand side of the cab, and thankful that he no longer had to swing the shovel around. As they left York on their way to Harrogate, Bill sat with his right hand on the regulator, gazing out of the cab, watching for signals on a pleasantly warm April morning. Apart from the war, the rationing and the poor pay, all was now right with the world.

Bertie was carefully checking the gauges, to keep steam pressure steady for this relatively short but demanding trip. Six non-corridors on the hilly run to Harrogate was going to push both the locomotive and its fireman. Bill watched his mate, busy with work that had been Bill's own until a month ago. He decided, in a moment of unusual generosity, to give his fireman a bit of a break and said, "You keep the shovel going, Bertie, and I'll watch for the signals." Bertie nodded his thanks; it took a load off his job and enabled him to concentrate more on firing the somewhat recalcitrant locomotive. He was pleased that his driver was assisting him so that he could concentrate on keeping a balance between sufficient heat for the steam pressure and yet not too much for the fire dropper in Harrogate. He knew that the engine would be stabled there overnight, and would not be welcome in the shed with a box full of fire.

Bertie looked up ten minutes later after he had checked to fire once more to see his driver smiling at him, then he glanced out of the cab through the front window, forgetting that his driver had promised to check for the signals. But what he noticed shocked him to the core. The rear lamps of a goods were approaching as they hurried towards it.

"Mr M!" he shouted. "There's a goods directly ahead of us!"

"What!" Bill stared out of the cab side, easing down the regulator as he did so, and applying the emergency train brakes, while Bertie turned the engine brake on. The speed of their train was such that, while Bill was able to slow it, he could not bring it to a stand before it hit the preceding goods train, derailing the brake van and several wagons.

Both Bill and his mate were badly shaken, but the guard of the freight suffered a more serious injury: he had been knocked off his feet and had a broken arm. None of the passengers on their train were seriously injured, but they were all assessed by medical staff called to Harrogate station, when their train was finally brought in by the Harrogate Station pilot engine. Under pre-war circumstances, Bill would have faced immediate dismissal from the railway. A SPAD, Signal Passed At Danger, was a very serious matter, but LNER managers were so badly short-staffed that they could not afford to lose a trained engineman, and he was kept on.

Nevertheless, Acting Driver Murgatroyd of York North shed was reclassified, and would be known again as Fireman Murgatroyd.

14 - A costly celebration
(May 1945)

As a boy in the mid-twenties, young Gerry Marston from Rickmansworth was mad keen on trains. At thirteen years of age, he already had an impressive Hornby clockwork train set, but on his fourteenth birthday he was presented with a dilemma. On a paternal visit to Gamages in London, his father had bought him an electric engine. It was a bright red Hornby *Royal Scot*. Gerry was almost in tears of joy when he saw it; he knew, of course, that Hornby's *Royal Scot* looked nothing like the LMS engine of the same name. He also knew that it looked exactly the same as Hornby's LNER's *Flying Scotsman*, GWR's *Caerphilly Castle* and the Southern's *Lord Nelson*, they only differed in their tenders and colour schemes. He even knew that it was based on the tooling for a French Hornby 4-4-2 class engine. His dilemma lay in the need to save his pennies and buy some electric rails for the engine to run on; all his rails had been for clockwork trains, which naturally did not need the third centre rail.

Like several of his school friends, Gerry spent many Saturdays at Watford Junction, watching the LMS expresses hurrying through the station hauled by Bowen-Cooke's Claughton class 4-6-0s and the ex-Midland Compound 4-4-0s, with an occasional sight of a Hughes Dreadnought class 4-6-0s. With their dark red coaches and matching engines, these were a constant delight to the youngsters who observed them; one which was considerably enhanced by the later appearance Fowler's Royal Scot class 4-6-0s.

A year after his fourteenth birthday, Gerry joined the LMS as a trainee cleaner at Camden shed. Camden was responsible for supplying the locomotives for most of the expresses leaving Euston for the north. Here, he soon heard enginemen's comments about the dearth of really good engines for their work. Only the Royal Scots seemed to meet with ungrudging approval for the heavy Scottish expresses, although the slightly smaller Patriot class 4-6-0s were well thought of for the lighter expresses.

The ex-LNWR Claughtons and the ex-L&Y Dreadnoughts were beginning to show their age, and the works at Derby and Crewe appeared reluctant to look into the matter, apparently preferring to build more of the ex-Midland Compound 4-4-0 locomotives. These were undoubtedly good engines, but they lacked the power needed for the heavy Scottish expresses, and management attempted to solve the problem by double-heading the trains. With the ever-increasing weight of these trains, what was really needed was a much more powerful class of engines. The problem was solved in 1932, with the head-hunting from the GWR of William Stanier, whom Lord Stamp empowered to override resistance in the LMS and who set about rejuvenating the LMS locomotive fleet.

Gerry's enthusiasm for railways did not suffer at all, even in his first weeks as an apprentice cleaner. He suffered all the jokes, tricks and indignities, which were the lot of new lads everywhere, taking them in good part and with a ready wit. He rapidly discovered that being a cleaner did not limit him to cleaning duties; he was required from time to time also to assist in carrying tools for fitters, firing the stationary boiler, shovelling ash into wagons for disposal, and brushing down the insides of a firebox. This latter job was not easy for a portly youngster, climbing into the fire-hole of a small tank engine removed waistcoat buttons quickly, but the duty had its compensations on a cold winter's day. Nevertheless, Gerry was once overheard by the passing Charge-hand Cleaner, Harry Edwards, as he was asking Jamie, another apprentice cleaner, to exchange jobs.

"What's the problem, young Marston?"

"Oh – er - nothing, Mr Edwards."

"Nice place, a warm firebox on a cold day like today. I'm surprised you don't want the duty."

"I thought you might suspect I was in there for a quiet fag, sir," said Gerry quickly racking his brains.

Harry looked at Gerry's waist. "Getting sort of prominent about the middle, aren't we?" he remarked.

"Well, er, yessir."

"Have you ever seen a fat fireman?"

"Fat fireman? No, sir."

"Nothing to worry about, then. You'll be a fireman, one day, if you work at it." And the charge-hand cleaner stalked off, smirking at his own wit.

Gerry waited until the man was well out of earshot, then muttered to Jamie, "Sarky bugger!"

In fact, for Gerry, 1932 was a year of promise; he had been a formal cleaner for two years, and Mr Edwards was showing approval of his progress. One morning in early May, when Gerry was cleaning the boiler of a general purpose ex-L&Y 2-6-0, when Mr Edwards called him down.

"A word with you, Marston."

"Sir?"

"Are you familiar with the enginemen's handbook?"

"Not as much as I perhaps should be, sir."

"Get hold of one and start studying it." And he walked off, leaving Gerry staring at his disappearing figure.

"What was that all about?" Gerry asked Jamie.

Jamie shook his head sadly at his friend. "Tell me, Gerry, why would anyone study the handbook?"

"It's the way to get promotion to Fireman."

"Exactly!"

"So?"

"D'you want me to spell it out? He wants you to go for the fireman's exam, you lucky sod."

"Blimey!"

In 1937, Gerry was promoted to Acting Fireman, and he began to really enjoy his life in the cab, because Chief Mechanical Engineer William Stanier's efforts to rejuvenate the LMS locomotive fleet was beginning to pay dividends. He had begun by putting superior Great Western-style tapered boilers into Hughes-designed L&Y 2-6-0s built in Crewe and Horwich. These engines proved to be very serviceable, and were the forerunners of his phenomenally successful Black Five 4-6-0s, believed by many to be the best general purpose engines ever built in Britain.

It wasn't long before Gerry was formally confirmed in his position as Fireman, and he began his firing duties mostly on tank engines taking short local freights between Willesden Junction and Camden Town and down the main line as far as Tring or Bletchley. But now that his pay had increased, another topic began to manifest itself. He had never invited a girl out, but when his mates began to boast of their (largely fictitious) conquests, this began to change. In the following few years, there were a number of young ladies with whom Gerry forged relationships, but none of them showed any signs of developing further, and his railway work was becoming increasingly arduous.

During the war, he was more involved in passenger firing duties and longer firing turns. He was now sometimes firing on the bigger expresses as far as Crewe, with occasional runs even to Liverpool or Manchester, and consequently had little spare time. He became familiar with the cabs of Stanier's new 4-6-0 classes: Black Fives and Jubilees as well as Fowler's Patriot class, and he was waiting until he had built up enough experience to handle the huge Pacific 4-6-2s now being built. These were really impressive machines and the first series, the Princess Royal class, had proved themselves quite capable of handling the heavy expresses without problems as far as Crewe and even Carlisle non-stop. But the really revolutionary engines were Stanier's new Duchess class Pacifics. LMS management was delighted with their new locomotive classes; in half a dozen years, Stanier had caught up with (and many claimed, overtaken) Gresley's fine locomotive stud on the rival LNER.

Fireman Marston felt himself to be privileged to be part of this pinnacle of LMS achievement, and he took pains to try and increase his route knowledge and experience, in order to reach the envied position of driver of the Scottish expresses. He knew this was not a matter which could be rushed; it would take years of dedication, and he would not allow himself any serious distraction. He had a private ambition to see himself as a top-link driver by the time he was forty.

When war broke out in 1939, there was no question of Gerry joining the armed forces like so many of his friends. When he raised the issue with his boss, the Camden shedmaster shook his head emphatically.

"Fireman Marston, d'you seriously imagine I would agree to let any of my competent enginemen join the army? Don't ask daft questions!"

"Sorry, sir." Gerry walked away, flattered that he should have been described as 'competent'. This sounded promising.

The next four years, however, showed little promise: bombing attacks on railway targets, especially around London, but also Liverpool, Manchester, Hull and even distant Belfast, were frequent. Trains were machine-gunned by low-flying enemy aircraft. Then there was the problem of maintenance; periods between maintenance stretched out so that locomotives began to break down more often, over fairly minor matters. Cleaning too, was now rare; the beautiful blue and red streamlined stock of the pre-war trains was now, like most other stock, grimy, and freight engines, which had been black before the war, were now appearing in dirty grey. Indeed, the only really clean big Pacific was the red *Coronation*, which had stayed in the USA after a publicity visit in 1939 and hadn't returned until 1942. (Although the real '*Coronation*' was grimy blue and under repair in the UK, while the engine in the USA was the substituted *Duchess of Hamilton*.)

The optimism in the country began to increase as 1943 turned into 1944. There were clear signs of German defeat after the great battles of Alamein, and of Kursk in Russia, and the inexorable advance of the Anglo-Americans in Italy. But around London, the optimistic feeling was blunted by the new air attacks. Hundreds of flying bombs, called 'doodlebugs', began to fall and, while these could be shot down if caught in time, the V2s could not. These latter rockets came without any warning whatsoever, striking fear once more into Londoners. In some ways, the last months of the war were the worst, as impatience for the German surrender grew and finally came with Hitler's suicide.

On the day of victory, Gerry, who had been promoted to Driver two months earlier, pulled into Euston with a special from Bletchley. He leaned out of the cab of his 4F 0-6-0 to watch hundreds of delighted revellers heading along the platform in the direction of the Palace to see Churchill with the royal family. His fireman, having uncoupled, was on the platform dancing with two girls. Three more young ladies, one with a bright red beret, clambered into Gerry's cab and hugged and danced with him before two of them descended once more. The third stayed, kissing him with vigour and passion; she began to undo his belt, before an enraged voice from the platform called out, "Driver Marston, what the hell d'you think you're doing?" Gerry instantly removed her hands and looked down to see Platform Inspector Morrison furiously staring at him from below. The girl quickly descended and, brushing past the inspector, her red beret bobbed as she hurried away.

"Inspector Morrison tells me that you, Driver Marston, were engaged in an indecent act with a paying passenger in full view of the travelling public."
 "Not exactly, sir," replied Gerry, thinking quickly.
 "How 'not exactly'?"
 "The girl is my fiancée, sir."
 "Your fiancée is an LMS employee?"
 "Well – no, sir."
 "So she was a paying passenger."
 "Sir." Gerry decided not to his luck any further.
 The shedmaster paused to gather his thoughts, then said, "You have brought the railway company into disrepute. Look, we all feel like rejoicing after what we've been through, but some of us have enough sense to celebrate in private. You're a stupid sod, Driver Marston. Three days' loss of pay, now bugger off!"
 Gerry left, thankful that he hadn't been either demoted or even sacked: both a distinct possibility. On his way home he reminded himself to keep a sharp eye open for a girl with a red beret next time he arrived in Euston from Bletchley.

15 - A platform embarrassment (January 1949)

When the war ended in 1945, the new Labour government handed the railways back to their owners as agreed. What the government did not do, was give any serious compensation to the railways to repair the enormous damage the war had done to this vital industry service. As a result, the railway companies in the next two years were in dire straits. Infrastructure, such as offices, maintenance facilities, rolling stock and tracks was in such a parlous state that they could no longer maintain a service comparable to that offered in pre-war days. The decision was therefore taken to remove the railways from the private owners and place them in government hands. This was done on 1st January 1948.

To make the changeover as painless as possible, it was decided to keep the initial management structure close to that of the big four companies, until such time as a major revision could be organised. There were four 'Regions'; the LMS territory became the 'London Midland Region', the LNER area became the 'Eastern Region', the GWR became the 'Western Region', and the Southern the 'Southern Region'. Overall planning was done at British Railways headquarters at St Pancras station, which became widely known in railway circles as the 'Kremlin'.

To begin with, there was little change for enginemen, except that their locomotives began to appear in the new BR colours as they progressed through the paint shops. General passenger locomotives were painted in Brunswick green; heavy express passenger engines appeared in Caledonian blue; mixed traffic engines appeared in glossy black with lining, reminiscent of the old LNWR colours, and freight engines were in unlined black. There were interesting exchanges of railway company engines, to discover their various strengths and weaknesses on different routes. Mr R. A. Riddles was appointed to the Railway Executive, and was involved in the design of a range of locomotives suitable for most areas on the system. They were specifically designed for ease of maintenance, and to burn low quality coal, and were generally successful after they began to appear in 1951.

The first type to appear was the Britannia 4-6-2, an express passenger locomotive series. In East Anglia, they were welcomed as the best engines the local crews had ever got their hands on, but crews on the Western Region were less impressed; WR enginemen claimed that their own Castles, which were still being built, were perfectly satisfactory. A lighter version of the Britannias named after Scottish clans was introduced for Scottish services. There was also a variation of William Stanier's ex-LMS Black Five, and several tank engines based on successful designs of different companies, though outwardly all reminiscent of the earlier LMS 'family' appearance. (Riddles the designer had been an LMS man.) Many of the new BR classes were tested against comparable existing types from the previous private companies with varying results.

Shedmaster Edward Stimson of Cardiff's Canton shed had other matters on his mind than new BR engines; the British Railways colour scheme for locomotives was causing him what he felt was unnecessary grief. Since the war had ended four years previously, he had been trying to get his engines back into proper, regular maintenance and cleaning, but now he had to have them changing in colours. The new BR symbol showed a lion with raised tail astride a wheel (which was the cause of some ribaldry among enginemen regarding the effect of a high wind on the lion's hindquarters when moving backwards at speed).

He was musing at this extra annoyance when his Foreman Fitter came into his office, grinning. "Have you heard the latest from the BR comparison tests, Mr S?" the man asked.

"No, Jack," replied Ted Stimson, "what did the tests show?"

His chief fitter explained, "They were testing their new BR 2-6-0, you know: just like the one designed by Ivatt for the LMS a few years back. Paddington sent a Dean Goods for comparison." (The Dean goods engines were handy little engines, but they were fifty years old.)

"What was the result?" asked the shedmaster.

"Our ancient Dean goods beat the pants off it!" cackled the chief fitter.

Ted Stimson smiled. "Don't get your hopes up; it'll only be a minor fault. That little LMS 2-6-0 was a good design; they'll soon fix it."

Over the next couple of years, some of the new BR standard locomotives began to appear at his shed, including the Britannias; these were the first 4-6-2 Pacifics to appear since the GWR's experimental *Great Bear* of 1908. This engine had been the first 4-6-2 on a railway in the country, and had not been a success; it was converted to a 4-6-0 in 1924.

The Britannias were generally not popular among most ex-GWR enginemen. "They can't do anything our Castles can't do!" complained one driver after he had spent time on one of them. His view was shared by many other drivers on the Western Region, although officialdom suspected the dislike was based on the mere fact that they were left-hand drive as opposed to the Western's right-hand drive engines. The men at Cardiff, however, began to take a different view, after some of the Britannias had been sent there; the 'Brits' were less fussy about the quality of coal, and were easier and cheaper to maintain.

Driver Geoffrey Archer reached for the regulator as he heard his mate, Fireman Albert Hankinson, call out, "We've got the green!" He lifted it gently, and the Britannia drew the eleven coaches of the Paddington express out of Cardiff General Station passing the Castle which had brought the train from Paddington and was now backing towards Canton shed for turning and servicing before returning to London the following day. Driver Archer was a serious, god-fearing man, with a belief that most people's lives were far too frivolous. They would be fortunate, he often mused, if they ended in purgatory rather than in eternal damnation. The recent war had, he believed, been responsible for a shocking lowering of moral standards. He glanced at the platform of Newport as they paused; that girl, for example: she was kissing the sailor with her in full public view – and wearing trousers, for Heaven's sake! Had she no shame? And then there was his mate Bert, who had never been to church in his life; Geoffrey was fairly sure about that. He had almost given up trying to get Bert to see his evil ways.

They were now well into the Severn tunnel and heading for Pilning, and their Britannia was running comfortably; Geoffrey knew that many crewmen did not like these new engines, but he felt that were as good as the Castles he was so familiar with, and they had an added advantage of having more weather protection in the cabs. They even included a gate between the cab side and the tender. "Did they think we would fall out?" asked his fireman Bert sardonically when he first climbed into one; Great Western engines were not normally provided with gates.

"Cup o' char at Swindon, Geoff?" asked Bert now. They had a slightly longer stop there. Bert was a problem for Geoffrey; in spite of his degenerate ways, he was a very personable character, and an excellent fireman, and it was impossible to dislike the man. He had joined the navy, and had been captured by the Japanese and served on the Burma railway experiencing horrors that would damage any man, but he had nevertheless retained an irreverent sense of humour.

As Bert was swilling out his tea mug as they were about to leave Swindon, when a book slipped out of his pocket and fell to the cab floor. Geoff stared at it in distaste; it had a lurid cover, showing a bikini-clad young woman apparently about to be molested by a huge gorilla. Bert picked it up and shoved it back into his pocket as Geoffrey said, "Sometimes, Bert, I think you're sex-mad!"

Bert smiled as he checked the steam pressure gauge. "So? What's wrong with that?"

"It's obscene!" replied Geoff indignantly, "You should be considering the finer things in life."

"What finer things?"

"For instance, philosophy: what is the purpose of your existence?"

"Fine," responded Bert. He saw a commotion on the platform; they were not going to get the guard's green flag for a few minutes. "What do you think is the purpose of life?"

"It is, er, to help one's fellow man to live a healthier and cleaner existence." Geoffrey hadn't expected Bert to reply in a philosophical vein and didn't have a ready answer.

"Right," said Bert. "I can go along with that. Now tell me, Geoff, how did you get here?"

Geoffrey frowned. "You know that. I became a cleaner then I applied for -"

"No, that's not what I meant. I mean, how were you born?"

"My parents loved each other, and they married, of course."

"But," grinned Bert, "plenty of couples love each other and even sleep together, without having children. So; how were you born?"

Geoffrey went onto the attack. "Bert! You know the details perfectly well!"

"Your parents had a sexual encounter!"

"Don't be coarse!"

"What else would you call it? In any case, it's vital for human existence, and therefore part of your god's plan."

Driver Archer shook his head and gave up the argument; in any case, he couldn't think of a suitable rejoinder. Bert, to his credit, did not smile in victory, he liked his driver and didn't want to upset him.

"How do you like these Britannias, Geoff?" he asked.

Geoffrey thought about this for a moment or two, then replied, "I find them fine, Bert, once you get used to them."

The rest of their run was uneventful, although they were held up at Reading and were twenty minutes late getting away.

"We're going to have to run to try and make up some time, Bert," said Geoffrey. Bert nodded; he was building up the fire to give Geoffrey the steam he would need. Between Slough and Paddington, they were racing along at close to eighty miles an hour, before slowing down through the approaches to Paddington.

As they slowly steamed into the platform, Geoffrey stared ahead to judge his speed and distance to the buffers, and suddenly stiffened. "Bert, we're steaming into trouble! We've got company."

"What's up, then?"

"I can see a platform inspector, and three or four porters waiting at the end of the platform for us."

Bert looked out too. "You're right. That doesn't look good. They're putting up what looks like some kind of screen." They drew to a stop and the inspector could be seen examining the front of the engine and talking animatedly to the porters. He hurried to the cab and climbed in.

"Anything wrong, sir?" asked Geoffrey.

"Yes, Driver," replied the inspector. "You've run someone down. There's a male head and part of a torso jammed between the smokebox and the left wind deflector shield of your engine!"

The two crewmen were horrified as the inspector continued, "You are both relieved of duty as from now, and will be required to explain what you know of this accident, while investigations are made on the track between here and Reading. I've had the smokebox covered with a tarpaulin, so that the passengers won't see anything untoward."

"We were certainly speeding to make up time lost at Reading, sir, but we have no knowledge of hitting anyone."

"No, I don't imagine you would have. You will probably be offered some compassionate leave."

The two men nodded; they knew such accidents happened more commonly than the public was led to believe, and they were never publicised, but all enginemen knew about the problem.

After their interview, in which they were totally exonerated, Driver Archer and Fireman Hankinson returned to Cardiff, and were given three days' leave. The news had reached Canton shed and was discussed in detail, and often with gallows humour.

"You shouldn't have been driving a Britannia, Geoff. Wouldn't have happened on a Castle," said Jeremy Rees. "No smoke deflectors!"

"A bloke's napper on the front buffer beam?" commented Amlodd Powell. "Gives a new meaning to the term headlamps!"

16 - Len's luck runs out
(February 1951)

It is a curious feature of human life that for some inexplicable reason, a few people seem to experience a remarkably generous amount of good fortune; whereas others, for no reason that anyone can explain, appear to be deprived of this benefit. Why this should be is for the religious, or perhaps philosophers, to account for. 'Lucky' Leonard Huxley was neither.

'Lucky Len' had always been known as a fortunate driver; he had joined the Midland Railway in 1920, just before the railway grouping of 1923. He had, as a young lad, always been convinced that a railway career was his purpose in life. Born in London near St Pancras station, there had never been any other railway company for him than the Midland. He had long admired its Spinners and Compounds, regarding them as the most beautiful and most efficient engines on British railways. Enginemen of other railways, very naturally, disagreed with him – on occasions, violently. In fact, his only regret when he joined was that the beautiful condition of the rolling stock he remembered from his youth was no longer apparent. The Great War had seen to that. However, in spite of the condition of much of the railways, he was quietly delighted at the financial difficulties of the Midland's great rival, the proud London & North Western Railway. When the latter was forced to merge with the Lancashire & Yorkshire Railway (although the LNWR kept the name), his joy knew no bounds. It was even further strengthened in 1923 at the Grouping, when the locomotive side of the brand-new company, the London Midland & Scottish Railway, was dominated by Midland men. Yet, the chief mechanical engineer was George Hughes, an ex-Lancashire & Yorkshire man, but he retired after two years at the helm and was replaced by Henry Fowler, late of the Midland Railway.

Len was formally appointed as a cleaner at Carlisle Citadel early in 1923, just as the new LMS had been formed, and was proud to see it adopt the colours of the Midland Railway for its engines and coaches. He rapidly became familiar with cleaning the locomotives of all six previous railway companies which served Carlisle. These were the Glasgow & South-Western, the Caledonian, the London & North Western, the Midland, the North Eastern, and the little Maryport & Carlisle railways. Over the next few years, the ex-company colours of most of these locomotives gradually disappeared, to be replaced by the same familiar Midland red for the passenger engines, and black for the goods engines. As the older and run-down machines of most companies were slowly eased out and sent to the scrapyard, the LMS was left with a serious problem of dealing with the heavy Anglo-Scottish expresses. The big 4-6-0s - the Claughtons of the LNWR, and the Dreadnoughts of the L & Y - needed urgent investigation to improve their minor faults, yet neither received much attention. Instead, the expresses were sometimes hauled by two ex-Midland Compound 4-4-0s, under the dictates of the largely ex-Midland rule. These, fine engines though they were, were underpowered for this kind of work, and CME Fowler looked around for a new and more powerful design for his heavy express services. He contacted the GWR, but they refused either to lend him one of their Castles, or to hand over the drawings for one. The Southern too did not lend him one of their Lord Nelsons, at the time the most powerful express passenger locomotives in the country, but they did send him a set of drawings.

Fowler took these drawings, added a few Midland refinements, and sent them over to the North British company in Glasgow. Within a year, the LMS had what they needed: a 4-6-0 which was considerably better than the older Claughtons or Dreadnoughts. The new Royal Scot class was an immediate success, and Fowler set about authorising the design of a similar but smaller version called the Patriot class, for the lighter services. This engine too became very successful, although its origin was dubious. Fowler called it a rebuilt Claughton, in order to satisfy the demands of the LMS accounts department; but in fact, only the first two engines had a few parts from a scrapped Claughton; the remaining fifty locomotives were brand new, but were not accounted for in capital expenditure.

Len had been assiduous in his cleaning, and had been

recommended to read the firing manual, with a view to going for his firing exam. One morning in 1923, Len Huxley was sitting with his mates, having lunch in the sun, when a 4-4-0 Compound rolled slowly into the siding, where the group was sitting. The driver descended, and walked off, waving at the sitting cleaners; "Look after her, lads." he called with a grin and left. As he left, the locomotive began very slowly to move, and Len looked into the cab, presuming that the fireman was still inside it. But the cab was empty. "The driver's left her without putting the tender brake on," he gasped to nearby cleaners, as he ran over to the locomotive, clambered into the cab, applied the tender brake, and the engine came to a standstill.

"Hey, you! What the hell are you doing in that cab?" The shout came from an angry passing driver. "The engine was moving, so I applied the tender brake," replied Len fearfully; cleaners were not allowed on engines in steam, without permission from the driver.

In the shedmaster's office, the other cleaners corroborated Len's explanation. The shedmaster nodded and took no further action against Len; instead, the careless driver was reprimanded, and the shedmaster encouraged Len to consider training as Acting Fireman.

"Lucky bugger!" commented one of the other cleaners to Len as they left the office.

A year later, Len was formally promoted to Acting Fireman status, and he began to fire in the various busy shunting yards in the Carlisle district. His promotion to full Fireman came soon after, as he passed his exam. Now his duties included firing turns on goods trains north to Glasgow, west to Maryport and Whitehaven, south to Crewe, and east to Newcastle upon Tyne.

On a Crewe South yard freight one morning, his driver, Fred Allport, who knew of Len's liking for anything ex-Midland, said mischievously, "How do you like our old G1 0-8-0, Len?"

The G1 and G2 heavy freight locomotives had been the heavy goods engines of the old LNWR.

"It's not too bad, Mr Allport, for an engine from a company which didn't know how to build good engines!"

Fred Allport laughed. "Cheeky young devil! What would you want on this heavy goods, if you could choose?"

"A 4F, perhaps?"

"A 4F 0-6-0? Are you serious? They're useful engines, I'll give you that, but they couldn't handle our load."

"One of our Midland 7Fs could."

"If they're that good, why did they only build a few for the Somerset & Dorset, and none for their own system?"

Len did not know how to answer that; he had often wondered himself.

Fred continued, rubbing it in, "These G1s are lumbering old carthorses, but they can pull anything." In fact, the old G1s had proved so effective that the LMS itself had rebuilt many of them, thus extending their useful lives.

Len nodded and picked up his shovel.

By the outbreak of war in 1939, Len was a driver, and frequently on the heavily loaded passenger services between Carlisle and Euston. One very late evening in May 1941, he was departing from Barrow Station with a passenger train for Carlisle, when an air raid began. One of the enemy bombers, a Junker Ju 88, was hit by anti-aircraft fire, and set alight. The burning aircraft began to glide down towards Len's train, passing a few feet overhead and, clearly with its bombs still on board, blowing up in a nearby street. Len and his fireman, distracted by the noise of the bombs and checking carefully for the signals, were totally unaware of their near destruction. Only later the next day at the Carlisle shed were they informed of how close they had been to death.

Some five months later, on a southbound troop train just north of Preston, Len's train was attacked by a low-flying Dornier bomber. The gunner fired a long burst at the coaches, killing and wounding several soldiers and, coming round for a second attack, aiming at the engine. Len saw the bomb hit the track a hundred yards in front of the train, but it bounced off without exploding. He stopped in Preston for medical attention for the soldiers, to have the damaged coaches detached, and to have his locomotive, a Royal Scot 4-6-0, checked out for damage, before he could continue south. Nothing amiss was discovered, and the train continued on its journey.

The wartime years for Len were hard, as they were for all enginemen: long shifts, often without breaks; difficulties in the blackout conditions; food rationing; bombing of railway yards and other facilities. Carlisle was not a major Luftwaffe target, but Manchester, Birmingham and London were, and they were all places where Len frequently found himself. Nevertheless, his luck held out, and he remained uninjured, yet suffered at least two more near-misses in the bombing.

In his home shed at Carlisle, amid the celebrations of VE day, Len had reached the top link and his shifts were taking him to north to Glasgow on the Anglo-Scottish expresses, as well as south to Crewe or even Euston, with trains to both Liverpool and Manchester.

"Ye've done well for yerself, Len," remarked one of his driving mates, "Yer've come through t' War wi'out bein' clobbered, even though t' Luftwaffe tried several times to nobble yer."

"Yes, I've been a bit lucky," Len replied.

"An' now ye're on t' big Lizzies and Duchesses!" his mate chortled.

Len nodded; his work in the cab of these great engines was the most exhilarating of his career, and he enjoyed it immensely.

The 'Lizzies' were Stanier's first attempts to utilize his experience with the GWR King class engines, which he had been involved with. His next essay, the Princess Coronation class, popularly known as the Duchesses, were an improvement, and to many people the finest express passenger locomotives ever built in Britain.

After the war ended, the big four companies disappeared, to be replaced by the new regional divisions. The LMS became the London Midland Region of British Railways. At first, there was little difference from what had been done previously, but gradually new BR locomotives began to appear.

For Len there was relief at driving without fear of being attacked, and the half-dozen years after the war allowed him to enjoy peacetime driving once more. Then, one evening in the autumn of 1951, he was in the cab of a Jubilee class 4-6-0, speeding with a Glasgow to Manchester passenger service just north of Lancaster, when a light engine was routed into his path.

The Jubilee hit the light engine, killing both Len and his fireman, as well as the enginemen of the light engine. Several passengers in the leading two coaches were also killed or injured. One minute later, through a terrible stroke of bad luck, a northbound express ploughed into the wreckage, adding many more deaths, including two more enginemen. The final count amounted to 74 deaths and 112 injuries.

The accident was entirely due to a signalman's error; he had been suffering from infrequent mental blackouts, but had failed to report his condition to his doctor, for fear of losing his job. As a result of the enquiry, he was dismissed from railway service, and faced a term of imprisonment for criminal negligence. This was of course no atonement for 'Lucky Len'.

Driver Leonard Huxley had benefitted all through his life from a generous portion of luck, but it had finally run out.

17 - Ernie Parsons drops a plug
(November 1954)

Ernie Parsons was a keen railway cleaner and had joined the Great Western Railway at Birkenhead shed in 1943. He was too young for the army at seventeen, but he had distinguished himself as a corporal in the Air Cadets during the Blitz when he, with several others in his squadron, had volunteered to assist in the cleaning-up after an air raid. He had rescued a small child from a collapsing building. The news in a local paper had impressed the GWR, and his application to join as a trainee cleaner had been accepted with alacrity. He had at the time made clear that he would leave to join the army as soon as he was old enough to do so.

In 1944 he reached eighteen, the age when the army could accept him and, true to his word, he joined up to be trained as an infantryman, just in time to take part in the D Day landings in Normandy. He had believed some of the propaganda that he had seen, and so was later horrified to find that a soldier saw and even did things that shocked him badly. He discovered very quickly that an infantryman's simple choice was to 'kill or be killed'. His dislike of killing enemy soldiers was strong, but not as strong as his will to survive. He managed this, but his year's fighting left him a nervous wreck when he was demobbed in 1946.

"There's a lot of lads coming back, Ernie," said the shedmaster at Birkenhead, when he fronted up once more, "but seeing as you've done well for yourself, I'll give you back your old job. You were with us for less than a year, so you'll have to work your way up the ladder again, lad."

"Thank you, sir," replied Ernie. "I'll do my best."

But over the following months, Ernie often felt that his best wasn't always good enough; he tried hard to overcome his nervousness by working quickly. In the next couple of years, he tackled the whole gamut of cleaner's jobs: cleaning the worst of the collected grime from passenger engines (freight engines were rarely cleaned); shovelling ash from ashpits onto the trackside for disposal; assisting the fitters in their work, and firing the stationary boiler used for heating sand for the locomotive sandboxes. He was gradually learning to overcome his nervousness, and, as he was always conscientious, he was respected by his colleagues, so much so that by 1949 he was promoted to Passed Cleaner. This meant that he could act as a fireman on occasions, and sometimes fired on local passenger trains to Helsby or West Kirby, as well as on local freights. Two years later, he was transferred to Chester shed.

Chester's GWR shed was larger than Birkenhead's, and was responsible for supplying the crews for many of the passenger trains south on the main line to Paddington. Barry Tomlinson, the new shedmaster, had a team of well over 120 enginemen in addition to the 200 fitters, boilermakers, cleaners, and other ancillary workers a large shed needed. He greeted Ernie formally but distantly. Shedmaster Tomlinson was not liked, although no-one on his staff could claim to have been treated either badly or unfairly. The simple truth was that the previous shedmaster had been immensely popular, and Mr Tomlinson found his predecessor's shoes hard to fill.

By 1954, Chester's Western Region shed was at its busiest, with increasing traffic. People were recovering from the war, and business and prosperity were booming; summer holiday traffic made heavy demands and, more importantly, freight traffic too was increasing. By now, Passed Cleaner Parsons was spending most of his time firing on shunting duties, freights and local passenger services; these took him to Helsby, West Kirby, Wrexham, and, on occasions, to Ruabon and up the Dee valley to Llangollen. These runs were nothing very demanding, but useful experience, and he was encouraged to study for his Fireman exam.

His passenger train experience was generally limited to the big Prairie class 2-6-2T tank engines, and most of the Chester drivers were quite happy to have him as a mate. However, Ernie was still at times a little unsure of himself if he was on an engine new to him. One morning, when working with Driver Alf Williams on a Chester to Birkenhead local, their regular engine failed, and the substitute engine was a 4-6-0 Star class express passenger locomotive; an engine Ernie had not fired on before. The Star was very near the end of its life, and was due to return to Swindon for scrapping. Unfortunately for Ernie, Driver Williams had a mischievous nature, and he watched Ernie shovel more coal into the firebox without reminding him that Birkenhead was not far away, and that the fire-dropper in Birkenhead shed would not be pleased to have to empty a firebox full of fire; the exchange of language would be interesting.

They left their coaches in Woodside Station in Birkenhead, turned their engine on the turntable, and moved over to the siding, where the fire-dropper waited to climb aboard. Alf Williams began to climb down the steps from the cab, but paused with an anticipatory grin on his face.

The elderly fire-dropper stared into the firebox and then glared at Ernie. "You an' yer mate are takin' this engine back ter Wolverhampton, are yer?" he asked truculently.

"Er - no. I think it stays here tonight," replied Ernie hesitantly.

"No heavy Paddington express?"

"No."

"Well, where did yer bring 'er from?"

"Chester. She's a substitute for the 51XX we should have been given."

"So, 'ave yer got yer chestnuts with yer?"

"Chestnuts?"

"Fer the Guy Fawkes bonfire yer've built."

"What Guy Fawkes Bonfire?" Ernie was by now totally confused. Alf had reached the bottom step, and was sitting there helpless with laughter. The fire-dropper was only a small man, but he grabbed Ernie by the ear and dragged him to the firebox and pointed inside. "Fer the bloody great bonfire yer've built in 'ere, yer daft git!"

"Oh, er, sorry!" Ernie grabbed his lunchbox and hurried down the steps.

"'Ow the 'ell did yet get ter be a fireman?" called the fire-dropper as Ernie hurried away to join his mate.

It did not help Ernie's confidence that the episode spread round the shed with the speed of light.

In early 1955, a strong bout of flu was in evidence around the shed, and this caused havoc within the duty rosters. Shedmaster Tomlinson was a very competent man, and it wasn't often that he made an error, but he did one morning with Ernie Parsons. The roster had once again been upset by a couple of enginemen reporting sick, and substitutes had to be found urgently. One of the ill men was Fireman Geoffrey Cardew; mate to Driver Lance Hargreaves; they were booked to run a Birkenhead semi-fast to Wellington. The train was due in Chester in forty minutes, and Chester was to provide the engine as well as the crew; the train would reverse in the bay platform, and the Prairie would come off, and the County class 4-6-0 would back on.

Barry Tomlinson was agonising over who would be available to fire to Driver Hargreaves when he noticed Ernie Parsons walking past his office. He got up, opened his door, and called out. "Passed Cleaner Parsons; here a moment, if you please."

"Yessir?"

"Change of duty, Parsons. Get yourself over to that County and fire to Driver Hargreaves. You're on the semi-fast to Wellington and returning on the Barmouth to Birkenhead freight picking it up in Salop. Tell Hargreaves his regular fireman has just called in sick."

"Sir." Ernie walked over to the indicated County, and climbed into the cab.

"Hi Ernie; what are you doing here?" Lance smiled at him, and Ernie explained the situation.

"Righto, then let's get busy." Lance accepted the change without further comment. Ernie checked the firebox and added a couple of shovelfuls of coal, and they backed out of the shed, across the main lines, and into Number Two Bay, where they waited for their train's arrival from Birkenhead.

"This isn't a hard run, Ernie, we'll only have seven or eight corridors on; you won't have to do much heavy firing, except up Gresford Bank. After that, it's plain sailing most of the way." Their train entered Number Two Bay and they backed on, and Ernie climbed down to couple up. He was quite excited: he had never fired on a semi-fast before, and Driver Hargreaves was known to be a friendly and helpful mate.

But in spite of Lance's words, Gresford Bank was heavy going, and Ernie had to shovel harder than anticipated. Working the County proved to be more difficult than he had expected. Pulling away from Baschurch, he was having difficulties with the big engine; he hadn't fired a County before, and Lance was unaware of this. Ernie had previously only fired the smaller locomotives, apart from the incident with the Star the previous year, and this bigger engine was demanding much more coal than he expected. This kept him rather too busy to notice the water gauges. This critical error was revealed to both crewmen in spectacular fashion: a sudden explosion of steam into the firebox, scalding Ernie on his hands and arms as he was about to put another shovelful of coal in.

"Christ, Ernie, you've dropped a plug!" yelled Lance, as he slammed down the regulator and rapidly eased the train to a halt. The lead fusible plugs were a safety device: they kept the boiler water and steam out of the firebox, as long as the water covered the crown plate over the firebox top. If the crown plate became uncovered, the firebox heat would melt the lead plugs and allow water and steam to enter the firebox, thereby quenching the fire before damage to the copper firebox.

Lance stared at his fireman. "Bloody hell, Ernie, how could you make such a basic mistake?"

Ernie was in too much agony to reply. Once the storm of steam had subsided sufficiently, his driver had to lift the firebars with a pricker to drop the fire and to put on the injectors to render the locomotive safe before he could help his mate. Driver Hargreaves had no alternative but to follow due procedure and fail his engine, and the train guard had to hurry to the nearest signal box to contact the signalman and tell him that the main line between Baschurch and Shrewsbury would be blocked until a relief engine could be sent from Shrewsbury, to tow the County and its train to Shrewsbury.

Fortunately, a doctor was found on the train, and was able to give professional aid to Ernie while they waited for the relief engines to arrive. Ernie returned to Chester 'on the cushions' with heavily bandaged hands, but Driver Hargreaves had to pick up an emergency fireman to help him man the rostered freight back to Chester.

It took three weeks' sick leave before Ernie could return to duty. The interview with the shedmaster was far less painful than Ernie expected.

"Not entirely your fault, Passed Cleaner Parsons," remarked Mr Tomlinson, "I was partly to blame for putting you into a position that you were not fully qualified for."

"And I should have checked your experience too, Ernie," added Lance.

Although the incident was noted on his record, there was no further action taken; and a very relieved passed cleaner left the office ready for his next duty.

"Our boss is not popular in the shed," commented Lance as they walked away together. "The lads have not yet all realised that Mr T's bark is worse than his bite. In my experience, he's a decent bloke underneath."

"Thanks, Mr Hargreaves, that makes me feel better!"

18 - Modernisation of the railways
(August 1955)

"Have you read this, Bill?" The Divisional Manager handed a copy of the Modernisation Plan to his chief clerk, when the latter entered his office with papers to be signed.

"Er - no, sir; what is it?"

"It's the BR Modernisation Plan - just came out this year."

"No, I haven't seen it, sir. What does it tell us?"

"First, Bill, how would you describe that board?" The Chief pointed to a bookshelf on the wall.

"Long, thick, made of wood, I suppose."

"Exactly! Describes the British Railways Board to a T. This document tells us, Bill, that we are managed by a group who take a long time, are thick, and have wood between the ears."

"How so, sir?"

"We are to be modernised. Steam locomotives are passé; they will be replaced by diesels, which British firms - with little diesel expertise - will build."

"But we are still building brand-new steam locomotives!"

"Certainly we are, and we will continue to do so, until the original order is complete. The last one is not due for completion until 1960, all of five years from now, and will be scrapped with fifteen years of life left in it within five or six years; the financial waste is extraordinary."

"Yet we do need a few more engines, sir, no doubt about that."

"I agree. But the old company workshops still have the drawings for their own engines; a few more of those would serve."

"Mmm. A lot of drivers will be very happy about the diesels. Conditions in a steam cab are not comfortable."

"The drivers will be, but not their mates: fireman will not be needed on diesel engines. And there's more: unprofitable branch lines will be closed, regardless of what the locals want. They aren't going to be happy. Put simply, Bill: our jobs are in danger, as well as those of half our enginemen."

"Good job you and I, sir, are close to retirement."
"Indeed. Now, hand me those papers to sign."

A mile or so away in the running shed in Carlisle, Driver Jake Andrews was delighted. "Just think, lads," he said, "in a few years I can sign on, walk to my engine, switch a lever, and three minutes later I'm off! Then after my shift my hands, shirt and tie are still clean."

"All very well for you, Jake," grumbled his young fireman, "but what about me?"

"You, Colin? You're always grumbling about shovelling coal into the firebox. You won't need to do that anymore."

"Well, what does a fireman do in a diesel? Tell me that."

"Ah yes, you may have a point there. You'll have to work on promotion quickly, or look for a new job."

Loud grunts of agreement could be heard from the younger enginemen. There were not too many who relished the hard and dirty work on the footplate, but the young firemen could see their jobs disappearing.

Driver Josh Fitzroy from York North shed, sat quietly listening; he was in a minority here, he thought. He was a senior driver in his fifties, and he enjoyed the exhilaration of powering a dozen coaches non-stop between Kings Cross and Edinburgh, through Doncaster and York, driving one of the Eastern region's big Pacifics - *an A4 for preference*, he added to himself. The relief crew would come into the cab through the tender corridor, halfway along the route, and then he and his mate could retire to the reserved compartment in the first coach. The streamlined A4s were the pride of the Eastern Region fleet; they were introduced by Sir Nigel Gresley before the war, and one of them held the world steam locomotive speed record of 126 mph. Gresley's successors, Thompson and Peppercorn, had continued building and improving on Gresley's work. Josh knew that other drivers shared his enthusiasm; he had once taken a special to Crewe, and a Crewe North driver had taken him (illegally) in the cab of a Duchess class 4-6-2 to Carlisle. He had been deeply impressed by the remarkable power of the big engine over the hills in Cumberland, and yet at the same time was wondering how one of his A4s would manage over Tebay on this hilly route; the East Coast Main Line was far easier. He also knew that most drivers did not share his feeling; most resented the difficulties of the job, the constant grime, the physical effort sometimes needed, and the necessity for arriving for duty an hour before you could move. In a diesel or an electric, you could climb in with a clean collar, switch on, and minutes later you could move off; then after your shift go home still with a clean collar. There was no comparison. He wondered whether he could stay a steam driver for the next ten years before he retired, or whether he would need to retrain as a diesel man.

Some weeks later, back in York, Driver Fitzroy was easing his streamlined- Pacific A4 4-6-2 back onto a Kings Cross train and was just passing the standing A4, which had brought the train from Edinburgh. He saw who the driver was and called across to him grinning. He knew that Jaimie MacIntosh was a fervent steam man like himself, but couldn't resist a quick tease as they passed each other.

"Have you booked on for your training for the diesels yet, Jaimie?"

"Nae, Josh, Ah hav'nae, but ah weel the minute yer book on yersel'!"

Snap! thought Josh with a smile as he nudged the locomotive's buffers gently against the train, for his fireman to couple up. Then he recalled a sight which had surprised him one morning in Glasgow. He was not often there, but on this occasion he had seen the coaches of an express for Euston waiting for their locomotive: a Duchess pacific, he had assumed, but had been very surprised to see two large black diesel engines backing on to double-head the heavy train. On the guard's signal, they had pulled away with what seemed to him to be impressive ease, which made him think again about what these main line locomotives could achieve if developed.

These thoughts were further supported when he visited a cousin in Oldham one weekend. He had travelled from York to Manchester Victoria Station to discover that his Oldham train was a green diesel set – multiple units each with an under-floor motor and gearbox. It felt very peculiar for a steam man to reach the end of the platform and hear the train change gear like a car! The open front of the coach permitted the passengers to get a good view of what the driver himself could see; and the thought crossed his mind as to whether one day in the not-too-distant future he would see women drivers on these new trains. The run to Oldham, although short, was smooth and pleasant, although he put this down, at least partly, to the newness of the vehicles. He wondered what they would be like when they had been in service for several years.

Much further south, unbeknown to Driver Fitzroy of York, Driver Harold Lawson of Stratford Shed in east London was also impressed with his steam locomotive; but in his case a new Britannia 4-6-2 after years of B1, B2 and B17 4-6-0s. While the 4-6-0s had been generally satisfactory for East Anglian services, the new Britannias were another matter altogether: they were magnificent, and Liverpool Street drivers loved them. Harold and Fireman Frank Barcham were preparing their charge to back down to the station to take the 'Day Continental' from Liverpool Street to Parkeston Quay in Harwich, where passengers would board the ferry for the Hook of Holland. This was not an unduly difficult service, but it was a heavy train with a non-stop run of an hour-and-a-half. Passengers on the train also needed to have booked tickets for the ferry to the Hook, where they could board trains for Holland, Germany, Scandinavia, and even for Poland and Russia. The various languages kept the stewards in the restaurant car on their linguistic toes.

Both Harold and Frank particularly enjoyed this duty; they were happy in the cabs of steam locomotives (with a few exceptions), although Frank was concerned about the future of firemen. They both lived in Harwich and were based in Parkeston Quay, and had worked together for several years, believing that they had the makings of a good team; an opinion shared by a good many of their colleagues in the shed. They were often rostered on the ferry trains, the 'Day' or 'Night Continental', or the 'Scandinavian' between London and Harwich, and the Stratford shedmaster Ron Shaw insisted on using the Britannias where possible for these services.

Harold was enjoying a quick cuppa in the mess shed when Frank appeared and sat down beside him. "We've got a Brit again, Harold, on the 8.20."

Harold was pleased. "I thought Ron said that we'd have a B1 today; he didn't have a Brit spare for us."

"I dunno about that, but the engine number on the listing starts with a seven zero!"

"Brilliant! It must have come back earlier than from its 'sole and heel' than Ron expected."

"It'll be in good nick, then."

"Yep, sounds like a good day. Out on the 'Continental' and back after lunch of the 'Scandinavian'; and they pay us to do this!"

"Aye, but not too much!"

The two men picked up their gear and moved out to the shed, to prepare their locomotive. Their departure from Liverpool Street was punctual at 8.20, and they were able to pick up some speed through the East London suburbs, running parallel to the electric trains to Shenfield.

"We'll be seeing the electrics as far as Chelmsford very soon, Frank," remarked Harold to his fireman. "I've already seen some of them running testing and driver training that far."

"Yeah, but it's taken long enough," commented Frank, shovelling more coal into the firebox as he spoke. "I remember 'em starting it when I was a cleaner more'n seventeen years back."

They concentrated on their work in the cab for a while; with their usual easy teamwork. They were slowing down to pass through Manningtree where the Harwich line diverged from the main Ipswich and Yarmouth line, and Harold grunted, "There's those kids on the footbridge again. Little buggers are always trying to drop their sandwiches down our chimneys. I've warned the stationmaster a couple of times, but nothing seems to happen."

But Harold spoke too soon; this time, something did happen. One lad, holding a sandwich to drop it down the passing chimney, lost his grip on his school satchel, which dropped neatly into their chimney, partly blocking the exhaust. The results were dramatic: it caused a blowback, as the sudden reversal in air pressure blew some of the fire back out of the firebox and into the cab. Both Frank and Harold received burns, but Harold had enough presence of mind to shut off steam, and apply the emergency brake. Frank, on the other hand, was more badly affected; his whole side was scorched. A porter on the platform saw the incident, and raced for assistance as the train slowed and came to a rapid and unscheduled stop in the station.

Within minutes, both enginemen had been given first aid, and were on their way to hospital. The boys on the footbridge, who had not understood what they had inadvertently done, were being interviewed by police. An emergency call to Parkeston Quay, resulted in a spare crew being sent to assist the Britannia piloted by B17 4-6-0 over the final few miles to Harwich.

Harold returned to his duties after his recovery, but Frank did not recover and died a week later. One of the younger firemen eager to undertake diesel training muttered quietly to another one, "Wouldn't have happened on a diesel!" He was right, of course, but in his later career he was badly hurt when at high speed a large bird flew into the windscreen of his diesel locomotive and filled the cab with shattered glass.

19 - A problem with homework
(April 1962)

The Herrman family were sitting quietly at home in Wittenberg one evening in early March; the crocuses were out in their tiny garden at the back of the house, and Frau Herrman had just that day been shopping and had been fortunate to acquire five oranges from the HO before the small shipment had been sold out. She was delighted at her luck.

The HO, or Handelsorganisation, was a kind of supermarket which the Communist authorities in East Germany boasted could supply the country with cheap goods, unlike the 'high prices demanded in the western part of the country by the rapacious capitalist companies', they reported. They could easily justify their claim by pointing out the differences in price of comparable goods in East and West. What was not mentioned was the fact that in West Germany, the East German mark was only valued at a quarter of what the West German mark was worth. Furthermore, the HO could only rarely provide many of the items which West Germans could pick up in their local shop any day of the week. Nevertheless, Frau Herrman was pleased at the unusual luxury available this evening to her family.

Driver Dieter Herrman popped the last segment of the orange into his mouth, sat back in his armchair, and glanced fondly at his children. Both Harald aged eleven, and his eight-year-old sister Heike had polished off their oranges, washed their hands, and were busy with their homework.

"Well, Harald, what have you got for homework today, my boy?"

"I have an essay to write, Papa. My favourite film."

"And you, Heike, my pet?"

"We have to draw a picture of our house, Papi."

"I'm glad to see that you are taking your work seriously, children," said their father. "It's important to do well at school."

Frau Herrman smiled. She was pleased to see her husband in

a good mood. His work at the local railway shed was not always easy as he sometimes had to put up with firemen who had strong political views. Talking politics was fine if you agreed with your colleagues, but dangerous if you didn't. You had to watch what you said all the time. A word out of place could be reported, and get you into serious trouble with the authorities.

Driver Herrman was stationed in Wittenberg, and was often on the main line to the border at Schwanheide. The only train allowed to cross into West Germany was the Berlin-Hamburg Interzonal train, which was an express with a carefully vetted crew, who could be relied upon not to abscond. Dieter Herrman had refused to join the Socialist Unity Party, or SED, and was therefore not regarded as secure; only crewmen belonging to the SED were granted further promotion and privileges. Dieter's close friend and regular fireman, Heinz Rübenkamp, could also expect little or no promotion as he too had similar views on the government's policies.

The two men were booked on a morning local passenger to Schwanheide. They had arrived, and Heinz had uncoupled their class 78 4-6-4T tank engine from its train, with a twenty-minute wait before they were due to return to Wittenberg. The daily Interzonal train pulled in and stopped at an adjacent platform for the border inspection. It was hauled by one the big class 01 4-6-2s, an express passenger locomotive. These 01s had been introduced in the 1920s as the Reichsbahn's premier express locomotives and still hauled the main expresses in both East and West Germany. The East German class could usually be distinguished from its West German counterpart by their wind deflectors: the East German engines still had the larger Wagner deflectors, known widely as 'elephants' ears', whereas the Western engines had the newer, smaller, Witte deflectors. East German railways also kept their pre-war title of DR (Deutsche Reichsbahn) on the side, in contrast to the Western engines with their DB (Deutsche Bundesbahn).

The two men were sitting together on a platform seat, eating their lunch: a Thermos of coffee, with black bread, sausage and cheese sandwiches.

"I heard," remarked Heinz to his mate, "that we are getting

some of our engines with the new Witte windshields when they go into the works for their repair."

"Yes," replied Dieter, "about time too, they are better at keeping the smoke clear so that we can see where we're going!"

"I also heard," continued Heinz with a grin, "that the Brits are using them on some of their express engines. Fancy them copying a German design!"

"They don't always get it right," commented Dieter. "They have also copied the Bundesbahn's diesel V200, and made a cock of it." The West Germans had designed an excellent diesel locomotive in the V200. It was a powerful multipurpose locomotive, and the British had built a lighter version of it under licence, but their Warship class had been much less successful.

While they were chatting, they saw three border guards marching off a man with a briefcase.

"Poor bugger!" muttered Dieter. "Wonder what he's done?"

"Tried to get out of our Workers' Paradise, I bet."

"For God's sake, Heinz, shut your mouth! You'll get us into trouble if anyone hears you!" hissed Dieter.

"Sorry!"

"You should be. You should know better, you daft sod!"

The border guards and railway officials had by this time cleared the Interzonal train, the guard had whistled and waved his disc and the huge locomotive moved smoothly away, with its mixture of DR and DB coaches.

"Next stop Hamburg Hauptbahnhof, then Hamburg Altona," muttered Heinz wistfully, "I wish to god—"

"Yes," nodded Dieter. "So do I."

Dieter noticed some railway workmen moving on to the main line west, following the Interzonal train as it disappeared. He saw that they were platelayers, with track-working equipment. "What are they up to?" he wondered.

"It's a repair job," said Heinz, "One of the blokes told me this track is to be re-laid. The track we're on is to be out of commission for a couple of weeks."

At home three evenings later, Dieter looked at his children's homework assignments while they were eating their meal and suddenly stiffened.

"Dieter, what's up?" asked his wife.

"Look at this, Elke," he said, pointing to the assignment in Harald's exercise book. "My favourite TV show."

"So? What's wrong wi... Oh!" she paled. "He loves 'Sesamstraße'; it's on West German TV! They're using the kids to spy on us!"

"I'm bloody sick of this," he snarled, "We're getting out!"

"But how? All the borders are mined and guarded!"

The next day, Dieter asked his fireman, "Listen, Heinz. How many people, apart from your family, can you be entirely sure of?"

"What do you mean?"

"How many will keep their gobs shut?"

"Not many; perhaps half a dozen. Why?"

"You want to go to the West?"

"You're damn right we do!"

"In three days' time, we're booked again on the Schwanheide local. Get those you can trust on it, but make sure they don't have loads of luggage. Only one small case each, otherwise the officials will smell a rat."

"How will we get out?" Heinz asked. "The platform points will be set against us."

Dieter thought for a moment, then said, "Leave that to me; and warn your friends, it might not work. They are to be prepared to return to Wittenberg if it doesn't."

"Mmm... it's a bloody dangerous risk!"

Dieter nodded; "It is; if they catch us, I'd be shot, you'd get ten years, and our families and friends would suffer for a long time. You know what the Stasi is like."

"What about the guard?" asked Heinz.

"I've looked at the schedule," answered Dieter. 'It'll be Ulrich Schabe."

"Schabe's a bastard. He'd report us instantly."

"He won't know till it's too late."

Three days later, early in the morning, the local Schwanheide passenger had a few more passengers than usual, but Guard Schwabe gave the matter no obvious concern on their departure. This time, Dieter and Heinz had an elderly P8 4-6-0 as their locomotive, but neither worried unduly; the P8s were reliable engines, and well respected by most enginemen. They were originally built before the first war and almost 4,000 had been constructed. Both East and West German railways ran them, although in the West they were often referred to as the 38 class.

Heinz checked the platform for the Peoples' Police, widely known as Vopos, but none were evident. Life appeared normal. He nodded to Dieter. "Everything seems in order."

The run from Wittenberg followed its usual course, with passengers embarking and disembarking according to the daily pattern. Approaching the Schwanheide station, Dieter lowered the regulator, checking that the signal for the main down platform was clear. They would normally have been directed into the down local platform, leaving the down main clear for the Interzonal to pull in a few minutes later. Now that the down local track was being re-laid, they were using the down main, with instructions to back away as quickly as possible after disembarkation, to allow the Interzonal through.

Dieter put his hand back on the regulator. "Ready, Heinz?"

Heinz nodded.

The train was slowing down and, as they entered the platform, one or two doors were being opened.

Dieter lifted the regulator, and the train accelerated past astonished station staff, and the opened doors slammed again quickly. One of the staff hammered on the stationmaster's door urgently. "It's the Wittenberg local, sir!" he yelled. "They're buggering off!"

"What?" The stationmaster tore open his door to see the local hurrying past. He ran back inside and grabbed his phone.

In the cab Dieter called to his fireman, "Get down now into the tender, Heinz, we'll be passing the border towers, and the guards'll be shooting!"

"But what about you, Dieter?"

"I'll be joining you when I can!"

By this time, Guard Schabe had realised what was happening

and he ran through the coaches, shouting to everyone, "Down on the floor! The border guards may be shooting at the train!" Startled passengers began throwing themselves down.

At the border in the first guard tower, the phone rang and the guard there picked up and listened for a moment, then dropped the phone.

"Uwe!" he called to his colleague. "There's a train belting through. We are to stop it!"

"What? How? They want us to machine-gun a train?"

"We'll go for the locomotive and its cab."

They trained their guns at where the locomotive would pass when it came through.

In the cab, Dieter set the regulator and dived back into the tender, where he threw himself on the coal next to Heinz. "Keep your head down!" he shouted. "We're almost there." As he spoke, bullets sprayed into the cab, shattering some of the gauges, but having no effect on the speed of the train as the locomotive burst through the barrier gate and continued headlong before finally stopping a few kilometres short of Büchen in West Germany.

Dieter and Heinz climbed down onto the tracks, where a few puzzled passengers had climbed down, wondering where they were.

"I think we're in the West!" one passenger gasped looking around.

"If we are, I'm bloody staying here!" stated another. "West Germans give us plenty of help." As he spoke, a number of West German border guards appeared, to render assistance where it was needed, and to record details.

Guard Schabe appeared, trying to usher the passengers back along the track. "Come along, come along!" he called. "The traitorous engine crew have taken us into the Bundesrepublik! Back to the East German border, where we'll be safe!" But he only had limited success. Several passengers, shocked yet delighted to find themselves unexpectedly in West Germany, refused to return.

"Well, Elke," said a smiling Dieter, as his wife and children came up to him. "We won't have to worry about the kids' spying on us anymore!"

Heinz's little five-year-old was fearfully holding on to his mother when a West German border guard came over to him. "Do you like bananas, sonny?" he asked. The child nodded. "Here you are," and he gave one to the child. The guard turned to Heinz. "I'm from Dresden," he explained, "I got out five years ago. I know things haven't changed over there!"

20 - A mishap in the cab
(October 1993)

It had been twenty-five years since the last main steam-hauled British Railways train had run. By now, a number of small tourist railways had opened throughout the kingdom, manned by enthusiastic volunteers, many of whom were ex-BR drivers and firemen. Large numbers of steam locomotives had been saved from the scrapyards, and were being refurbished to run once more. Indeed, of the almost 300 locomotives sent to Woodham Bros in Barry, South Wales, for scrapping, more than 200 were saved. Most were bought either for repairing and running in tourist lines, or were bought to supply spare parts for other locomotives. Such was the interest in steam after its formal demise on the nation's government railways. Even BR kept its own narrow gauge Vale of Rheidol steam railway, painting the stock in the new colours.

Bill Harbison was a keen fireman in his early thirties, with the makings of a good driver, and was training on the North Yorkshire Moors Railway. His father had been a steam driver with BR, based at Crewe North shed. Young Bill had often been with his father on shed shunting duties and was, consequently, no stranger to a steam locomotive cab. An accountant by profession, he had joined the NYMR as a hobby crewman, with the intention of becoming a driver, and spent most weekends under instruction there. He had no family to support, and his other hobby was photography, at which he had won several prizes in local competitions.

After several years on cleaning and firing instruction, he had qualified as a fireman, and was now firing on an ex-GWR 0-6-2T Collett tank engine. His driver, Ted Pearson, had handed the regulator to him along a quiet stretch of the line, but had now taken the regulator back as they neared the next station.

"I've been watching you now, Bill, for a couple of weeks in

these holidays, and I reckon you aren't too far off taking your driver's exam." Ted said with a smile. "You've got the hang of firing, and it's time you thought of the next step."

"Thanks, Ted, for the encouragement. I've already been studying the driver's rule book." Bill bent to open the fire doors and check the fire. They were about to stop, and this would give him a chance to shovel coal in more accurately where it might be needed, while the locomotive was stationary at the platform. However, a quick glance showed that all was well, and he shut the fire doors once more. Along these short tourist lines with their easy timetables, firing was not usually an arduous task.

"By the way, Bill, I've heard that a new group of people are interested in joining the company, with a view to training as engine-men- er, people."

Bill looked at him frowning. "Engine-people? What d'you mean, people?"

Ted smiled and said, "Two of the newcomers are girls."

"Girls?" exclaimed Bill in shock. "What; girls as firemen and drivers?"

"That's what I heard."

"But how can girls fire? The coal can be bloody heavy!" The swearword slipped out. Bill was, unlike most crewmen, not prone to strong language. He thought about the matter. "I know they had women on the railways in the War," he said, "even as guards, but not in cabs – they couldn't do the job!" Bill was very unsure of himself where females were concerned; he had been strictly brought up to believe that women were the source of most male problems. They drove men to drink (Bill was a teetotaller), they broke up marriages, as he knew; his own mother had left his father for a postman when Bill was seventeen. In short, they were creatures to avoid wherever possible. Bill had so far successfully avoided contamination, and he emphatically didn't want to see any members of this Satanic brood in any cab he was in.

The whistle sounded, and Ted lifted the regulator gently as Bill, with such thoughts in his mind, thrust his shovel angrily into the coal bunker and threw the shovelful into the firebox. He turned and hurled another two shovelfuls in as Ted stared at him.

"Take it easy, Bill!" said Ted. "We've already got enough steam before the next station."

"Sorry Ted, I don't know what I was thinking of."

"Well, think of how powerful these Collett tanks are, and how much steam we need to reach Pickering!"

Bill nodded sheepishly. "Of course." He stopped shovelling, and checked the gauges carefully.

On reaching Pickering, Bill climbed down to uncouple the engine from its train, so that Ted could ease forward across the release crossover and back down to the other end of the train to take it back to Grosmont. Bill strolled down the platform, answering the occasional question from the holiday passengers as he went, before dropping down again onto the track to couple up as soon as Ted backed his engine to gently nudge the buffers into their shanks, so that Bill could then lift the coupling hook over, tighten the screw to couple up to their train, and link the steam brake pipes.

On climbing back into the cab, he was surprised to see two other people chatting to Ted. One was the chief crew trainer, but the other was a slim girl; in her twenties, he judged. She was dressed in none-too-clean jeans, and a t-shirt with oil stains on it.

"This is my fireman, Bill Harbison," said Ted to the girl. "He'll show you how to fire – he's very good at it – usually," he added with a grin at Bill. "Bill, this is Annie," he continued, "she's coming back with us to Grosmont for you to show her how to fire an engine!"

Bill looked doubtfully at the girl. She was rather slender to shovel coal. Those arms did not suggest strength, although her t-shirt was disturbingly filled, and he turned his eyes away quickly in embarrassment.

She held out her hand to him, smiling. "Hello, I'm Annie," she said, "I'll try not to distract you. I'll just sit on this little shelf and watch, if that's fine with you." Bill just nodded; she was attractive, and a distraction by just being there. But if that's all she was to do, well, he could live with that. In fact, she did exactly what she said she would do, and observed him on the run to Grosmont, noting when he fired, when he glanced into the firebox, when he checked the steam pressure, and when he observed the signals ahead.

Both men came off duty at Grosmont and Annie shook Bill's hand and thanked him for his patience. "I'm looking forward to another demonstration very soon." Bill sent an enquiring look at Ted, who said, "Yes, Annie will be with us several times next week."

Bill drove home, wondering how this was going to affect his work in the cab. He had always been careful to keep his distance from females, but this was impossible in a cab. Over the next few weeks, Annie was frequently in the cab watching him; he even let her handle the coal shovel occasionally, and watched approvingly as she directed the coal into the corners as he had shown her. There was no sign at all of her finding the work too heavy.

Soon, another matter occupied Bill's mind: he was preparing to take his driver's exam. He concentrated hard on both the theory and practice exams, and was rewarded with his driver's certificate shortly after. For a while he was driving with Ted Pearson as supervisor and Jack Finch as fireman. Some months after this, he was driving without supervision, and with Jack as his regular fireman. He and Jack got on well, but Bill found his mind turning to wondering what it would be like to have Annie firing for him. He hadn't seen her except at a distance once or twice in the intervening months, but he had heard that she had been learning to fire.

A year or two, later Bill achieved one of his ambitions: he was rostered to drive *Repton*, the Southern Railway's Schools class 4-4-0. These engines had been one of Richard Maunsell's most successful designs, and were also reputed to be the most powerful 4-4-0s in Europe. Bill had long wanted to drive one, and was delighted to see his name on the list. Looking further along, he was surprised to find that Annie had been rostered to fire to him. She must have passed her firing exam. She arrived in the cab, greeted him with obvious pleasure, and began checking the fire and the various gauges. Bill's doubts began to dissipate; the girl was clearly competent in her duties, and he found to his surprise that he actually enjoyed her company. Furthermore, now that she was dressed in a fireman's overalls, he was no longer distracted by her tight t-shirt, which he recalled with some misgiving.

The August holiday week was for Bill one of the most pleasant weeks he had ever spent on the railway. Annie handled her duties very competently, and was additionally an entertaining companion. But an incident halfway through their second week brought an abrupt change to the easy relationship.

It was a warm day, and as Bill walked in to book on duty, his mind was so full of anticipation of another enjoyable day that he missed a notice on the door of the men's changing cabin. The female staff changing room had been damaged by fire overnight, and they were temporarily given the use of the men's room. Men were asked to change in the little office at the back of the engine shed.

On entering the changing room, Bill was confronted by the back of a near-naked female who was wearing only a pair of briefs. On hearing the door, the girl turned round, and Bill saw that it was Annie. She stood there with arms akimbo, and a half smile on her face.

"Naughty, naughty, Bill; you really shouldn't be here!" she said with a grin. Bill's eyes boggled and his face took on a beetroot-like hue as he turned and fled. He distinctly heard a chuckle as he shut the door behind him.

Bill was waiting in the cab of *Repton* on the turntable as Annie climbed to join him. She was wearing shorts and a t-shirt. "Too hot today for overalls," she remarked, as she peered into the firebox and took hold of the shovel and bent to pick up coal from the tender. As Bill's eyes were glued to the t-shirt, watching its undulations, a shout came from below, as the shunter called out that the turntable was correctly lined up. Bill tore his eyes away and eased the regulator a little, to move the locomotive off the turntable and take it out into the station. The engine reversed gently off and onto the siding stub, where it hit the stopblock, pushing it over, before coming to a sudden stop. Bill had forgotten to put the engine into forward gear.

That morning, Bill was required to explain his error, and Annie said that as he had put his hand on the reverser, she had asked him a question, which had obviously distracted him, claiming the fault was hers. This was not accepted, and Bill was taken off driving for three months.

The next weekend, Annie appeared at Bill's flat with a bottle of gin. "I know you're a teetotaller," she said, "but this could really help." She wanted to apologize, she said; she felt terrible about the incident, and had enjoyed working with him. As the afternoon turned into evening, Bill's views about relationships with females began to change in inverse proportion to the level of gin in the bottle. By the time Annie had cooked his breakfast on the following morning, he was totally won over. Seven months later, they married, barely in time to ensure respectability for the arrival of their baby daughter.

Glossary of Technical Railway Terms

Banking engine: An engine at the rear of a train assisting by pushing from behind.

Bobby: railway signalmen. The name derives from Sir Robert Peel's police force. It was also used to refer to railway police. (see also 'Peeler')

Brake van: small van at the end of a goods train from which the guard could apply a brake to assist the driver when slowing the train. In a passenger train, the brake van would be a coach with a section for the guard.

Brighton Line: Railwaymen's term for the London, Brighton & South Coast Railway.

Broad gauge: Brunel's original seven foot (and a quarter of an inch) railway gauge for the Great Western Railway, finally abandoned in 1892.

'Coal miners' friend': a term used to describe a driver who was unnecessarily profligate with coal.

Distant: a signal warning drivers about the status of the section following the one they were entering. (see also 'home' and 'starter')

Driver: the man who controls the locomotive.

Down: the direction from London. (see also **'Up'**)

Express: A fast train with only limited stops.

Fireman: the man who ensures that the locomotive has sufficient energy for the driver to do his job. Earlier commentaries refer to the fireman as a 'stoker'.

Grouping: The Railways act of 1921 grouped the 120 railway companies into four main groups: the Great Western Railway, the London Midland and Scottish Railway, the London & North Eastern Railway and the Southern Railway.

Guard: the official in charge of a train; he was normally at the rear of the train.

Home: a signal indicating whether the next section is clear. (see also **'distant'** and **'starter'**)

Horsebox: a van specially fitted out for transporting horses.

Light engine: an engine travelling without a train.

Mixed gauge: A stretch of broad gauge track within which a third, standard gauge rail has been added to allow trains of both gauges to run. (see also **Dual gauge**)

Motion: the set of coupling and connecting rods linking the driving wheels and the cylinders.

Narrow gauge: Broad gauge enginemen of the GWR referred to the standard gauge as 'narrow.'

'On the cushions': Enginemen returning from duty and not required to drive a locomotive were permitted to travel in comfort with passengers.

Permanent Way: This is the track and its foundation, which need regular checking.

Pilot engine: engine which would be coupled in front of a train engine and used to assist with a heavy train.

Salop: railway term for Shrewsbury, based on the original Latin.

Semi-fast: a train which does not stop at all stations.

Single: a locomotive with one large driving wheel on each side.

Shunting: a process whereby railway vehicles were moved about to re-arrange trains. It took place in shunting yards and was done either with a locomotive or by using horses and ropes.

Starter: a signal (usually at the end of a platform) to indicate whether a train may move off to the next signal. (see also **'home'** and **'distant'**)

Stoker: see 'fireman'.

Stopblock: a structure at buffer height at the end of a track to prevent further progress.

Stopper: a train which calls at all stations on its run.

Turntable: a large, revolving table in an engine shed. It permits engines to be turned round.

Up: the direction to London. (See also 'down')

Collect all Steaming Into books:

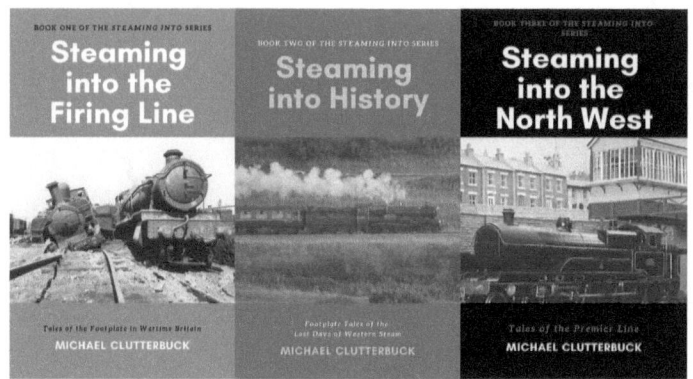

www.ingramcontent.com/pod-product-compliance
Lightning Source LLC
Chambersburg PA
CBHW021153080526
44588CB00008B/320